# YORK NOTES

General Editors: Professor A.N. Jeffares (*University of Stirling*) & Professor Suheil Bushrui (*American University of Beirut*)

## Sean O'Casey

# JUNO
# AND THE
# PAYCOCK

*Notes by Barbara Hayley*

MA (DUBLIN) PH D (KENT)
*Senior Lecturer in English,*
*St Patrick's College, Maynooth*

LONGMAN
YORK PRESS

Extracts from *Juno and the Paycock* by Sean O'Casey are reprinted
by kind permission of Macmillan, London and Basingstoke, and
St Martin's Press Inc., New York


YORK PRESS
Immeuble Esseily, Place Riad Solh, Beirut.

LONGMAN GROUP UK LIMITED
*Longman House, Burnt Mill, Harlow,*
*Essex CM20 2JE, England*
*and Associated Companies throughout the world.*

First published 1981
Reprinted 1989

ISBN 0-582-03089-7

Produced by Longman Group (FE) Ltd
Printed in Hong Kong

# Contents

# Part 1

---

# Introduction

## Sean O'Casey's early life

Sean O'Casey's autobiographical writings show him as an outsider, a fighter, and a man dedicated to learning. He was born John Casey in Dublin in 1880. Several facts combined to make him an outsider. First, his family was extremely poor, especially after his father's death in 1886. They lived in progressively poorer tenements, often with barely enough money to buy food. O'Casey describes his brothers and sisters sinking from promise to degradation through their poverty, and his mother, to whom he was devoted, dying comfortless after a life deprived of joy, beauty or rest. The Dublin of the poor was a city of disease and wretchedness: one-third of the population lived in single-room tenements with no heat, light or sanitation; the infant death rate was the highest in the British Isles; vast numbers were unemployed. The Caseys were Protestants, in a country and particularly a city where the rich were generally Protestants, the poor Roman Catholics, and the religious and social barriers between them jealously preserved. So O'Casey was isolated from his neighbours by his Protestantism and from other Protestants by his poverty. Another factor which made him an outsider was a disease of the eyes, trachoma, from which he suffered throughout his life: as a boy it was feared he would go blind; he could not attend school regularly or play with other children; he had to wear rag bandages on his eyes and was constantly in pain.

O'Casey the fighter overcame this handicap. His sister taught him to read at 14. He had a phenomenal memory and could memorise whole plays in which his brothers acted, and indeed he started his theatrical career by stepping as understudy into a part in Dion Boucicault's great Irish comic melodrama *The Shaughran*. His dedication to literature started in boyhood; he bought what books he could, stole a few, and read widely. He describes himself as having from an early age a dominating desire to have a play staged at the Abbey Theatre in Dublin. His career started, however, with a number of labouring and caretaking jobs which continued until he was 44; he was not a success with either co-workers or employers.

# Nationalism and socialism

Although a natural outsider, O'Casey was a joiner, and indeed an organiser, of organisations. From 1906 to 1914 he joined progressively more revolutionary Irish societies at a time of great political activity in Ireland. The two strands of revolution that drew him were nationalism and socialism; the starting point was his interest in the Irish language, which, having been commonly spoken in country parts of Ireland up to the early nineteenth century, had been replaced by English and was now practically obsolete. He joined the Gaelic League, a society for fostering Irish language and literature. He learnt Irish, and gaelicised his name to Sean O'Cathasaigh, the Irish for John Casey (as a playwright he partly anglicised it again to Sean O'Casey). He joined the Saint Laurence O'Toole Club and its Irish Pipers' Band; this was a social club whose pursuits such as Irish dancing often led on to more militant nationalism.

The nationalist background plays a large part both in O'Casey's life and in the settings of his early plays. Since 1800 (the year of the Act of Union with Great Britain), Ireland had been part of Great Britain with no independent parliament of her own, but with members elected to the British Parliament. For some time this parliamentary party (until 1891 led by Charles Stewart Parnell) had been agitating for Home Rule for Ireland—that is, the power of governing herself within the British Empire. Not all Irish people agreed with this aim—some, 'nationalists', wanted total independence and an Irish republic. Others, 'unionists', wished to continue the union with Great Britain. Irish nationalists were of two kinds—nationalists pure and simple who wanted an independent Ireland, and those who were more aligned with the Labour movement. Starting from an Irish interest, O'Casey became drawn more to world socialism than to Irish nationalism, though at that time both forces were working together for revolution in Ireland.

There were then two powerful figures in the Irish Labour movement: James Larkin, an impressive orator, and James Connolly, an effective theoretician. Larkin believed in the use of industrial power to overthrow the capitalist state; from 1908 he organised Irish workers into trade unions, and in 1913 initiated a general strike by withdrawing all his union members' labour from the Dublin United Tramway Company. The men were locked out by the employers; the lockout lasted for eight months, with 25,000 men out of work, causing great hardship and ending in failure. O'Casey supported the general strike. He was secretary of the Women and Children's Relief Fund that provided charity for the families of those locked out. Larkin, big, flamboyant, powerful, was one of O'Casey's heroes—he portrayed him as 'Red Jim' in his Communist play *The Star Turns Red* (1940).

Connolly also considered the Irish problem to be an economic one, but he felt that political rather than strike action would be needed to solve it; then society could be reshaped on socialist lines. He and his party wanted an Irish Socialist Republic founded on nationalism and public ownership; to them, private ownership was the cause of all oppression. By overthrowing the capitalist framework, they would be fighting for a people's republic benevolent to the working classes. The Irish Citizen Army was formed to train and equip Irishmen to fight for this democratic ideal. O'Casey joined it, and as Secretary helped to reorganise it in 1914, though he left it soon afterwards because he thought that some of its members were more committed to Irish nationalism than to world socialism. One of his first books was *The Story of the Irish Citizen Army* (1919), which includes his own part in it.

In 1914 the world war broke out—despite world socialism and its fraternal vows—and this was a great blow to Labour idealists. Connolly became more militantly nationalist, justifying an Irish revolution by saying that it might contribute to a general defeat of capitalism. Another prominent nationalist figure was Patrick Pearse, leader of the Irish Volunteers. He was an idealist, dedicated to education and to Irish language and literature. He thought the only serious nationalism was armed. For him the cause of Irish poverty lay in British domination; limited 'Home Rule' as proposed in the Bill passed by the British Parliament in 1914, but shelved until after the war, did not satisfy him. Others militantly opposed to it were the Sinn Fein party; the Irish Republican Brotherhood, heirs of the earlier Fenian rebels; and a military youth movement, the Fianna. These combined revolutionary republicans struck out against British rule in 1916. The Easter Rising, so seminal in Irish history and literature, took place on Easter Monday, 1916. For a few days the rebels held out, and Pearse read a proclamation of an independent Irish Republic. When the insurgents were defeated, after violent disorder, and shelling from a British gunboat, those involved were imprisoned and fourteen leaders were executed, including Pearse and Connolly. This is the background to O'Casey's *The Plough and the Stars* (1926).

Though the mass of Irish people had been indifferent or hostile to the insurrection (indeed 150,000 Irishmen were then serving in the British Army), the country was horrified by the executions, and its mood became more warlike; a cult grew up around the dead leaders as heroes and martyrs. The Sinn Fein party became the advanced nationalists.

They stood for election as Members of Parliament, and those elected formed a separate Irish Parliament in January 1919. The Irish Republican Army fought to enforce this independence; the British recruited auxiliaries, the hated and brutal 'Black and Tans', to help to put them down. They seized people in night raids, fired on civilians, and committed atrocities. This is the period of O'Casey's *The Shadow of a Gunman* (1923).

After a truce and negotiations in 1921, a treaty was signed giving Southern Ireland the status of a dominion with restricted self-government, to be named the Irish Free State. Some Irish saw this as a respite from war; others, the entrenched or 'die-hard' Republicans, saw it as a debasing compromise and determined to overthrow it. They, as 'irregular' forces, now fought not the British, who had gone away, but the legitimate Irish forces, in a bitter, bloody civil war. This guerrilla war, which did not end until 1923, is the setting of *Juno and the Paycock* (1924). Southern Ireland finally became a republic in 1948. The futility and waste of the civil war, and its failure to improve the life of the ordinary Irishman, are the principal themes of *Juno and the Paycock*.

# Early literary career

O'Casey's first full-length plays to be produced took for subject and setting the three critical periods in Ireland's recent history. *The Shadow of a Gunman* was set in 1920 when the Black and Tans were raiding; *Juno and the Paycock* in 1922 when the civil war was being fought, and *The Plough and the Stars* in 1916 at the time of the Easter Rising. O'Casey became a playwright at the age of 40 when he was still a labourer; he fulfilled his driving ambition to have a play staged at the Abbey Theatre when it accepted *The Shadow of a Gunman* in 1922, having rejected four others.

The Abbey Theatre had been founded by W.B. Yeats, Lady Gregory and Edward Martyn in 1898 as the Irish Literary Theatre, a vital part of that rebirth of Irish literature which came to be known as the Irish Literary Revival. The main aims of the theatre's founders were to rebuild an Irish dramatic literature, to educate the Irish public, and to establish a working theatre regularly staging plays by contemporary dramatists. The 'education' included classical plays and translations of European dramatists such as Ibsen, but was principally concerned with the rediscovery of Ireland's own culture, her literary, legendary and mythical traditions. The new plays produced there were of differing types: Lady Gregory's gentle comedies of peasant life; plays of social realism such as Padraic Colum's *The Land* or Edward Martyn's *The Heather Field*; plays about Ireland's Celtic or bardic history. Yeats himself had started with a parable of Irish nationalism, *The Countess Cathleen*, had gone on to Celtic mythological subjects, and was moving towards a stylised poetic drama based on the Japanese Noh theatre. The Abbey's greatest playwright so far had been John Millington Synge (1877–1909), who had written about peasants in County Wicklow and the Aran Islands off the Galway coast in the West. His plays were tragi-comedies written in vivid, lyrical speech, rich with images and echoes of Irish. His *The Playboy of the Western World* had caused a riot in the theatre because some of the audience thought the play had cast a slur on Irish womanhood—an objection raised earlier to his *In the Shadow of the Glen*.

Up to 1923, O'Casey had written magazine articles, *The Story of Thomas Ashe* (1918) and *The Sacrifice of Thomas Ashe* (1918), in honour of a dead revolutionary, and three collections of ballads, *Songs of the Wren*, I and II (1918) and *More Wren Songs* (1918) and *The Story of the Irish Citizen Army* (1919). In 1923 his two-act tragi-comedy *The Shadow of a Gunman* opened at the Abbey Theatre, a popular and critical success. Its main character is a poet, mistaken for a heroic gunman on the run. Tragedy comes when the girl who loves him shields him by taking some bombs that have been left in his room; she is shot by the Black and Tans. In 1923 the Abbey Theatre also staged O'Casey's one-act fantasy *Kathleen Listens In*, a parody satirising Irish political parties, to which the audience reacted with total silence. Not all his early plays were in the 'realistic' mode that people see in the three Dublin plays; elements of surrealism, parody and fantasy are already present in *Kathleen Listens In*.

In March 1924, *Juno and the Paycock* was produced at the Abbey. Its enormous success saved the theatre which was in a very precarious financial state. It ran for two weeks (an unprecedented run) to packed houses, and was extremely well reviewed. This was followed by *Nannie's Night Out* (1924), a one-act farce about a drunk woman out of prison for a night. In 1926, his four-act tragi-comedy *The Plough and the Stars* opened, to riots, rage and an unpleasant and protracted controversy. Its setting was Easter Week 1916, and the Rising; but its scenes were far from heroic. O'Casey showed the people of Dublin looting and stealing; he used Patrick Pearse's rousing speeches as a background to the destruction being caused to ordinary people; they are shot, die of consumption, lose their babies, go mad. This is far from the cult of the heroic sacrifice. The nationalists were furious at the idea of using the 1916 rising as material for an unheroic play, showing the Republican flag in a public house, and using Pearse's speeches; 'moralists' were outraged at the notion of an Irish prostitute. Yeats, who had defended Synge against a rioting audience, defended O'Casey similiarly: 'You have disgraced yourselves again ... Dublin has once more rocked the cradle of genius. From such a scene in this theatre went forth the fame of Synge. Equally the fame of O'Casey is born here tonight. This is his apotheosis.'

Even before this controversy, O'Casey had been feeling ill at ease in Dublin. In one of his autobiographies, *Inishfallen Fare Thee Well* (1949), he describes his years of being a successful literary man in Dublin, sought after and lionised. But he never stayed in any society for long, and left Ireland in 1926 to live in England. There was much criticism of this self-imposed exile: claims either that he had deserted his country, or that he had cut himself off from the kind of play that he should have been writing, that is, Dublin realism. But in fact there is a strong tradition of exile among Irish writers. Those of the eighteenth century, such as Goldsmith and Sheridan, gravitated to London as the centre of the literary world; in the nineteenth century, publishing and most literary activities flourished only briefly in Ireland. There were other good reasons for leaving behind the constrictions of Ireland—such things as the riots directed at Synge and O'Casey, the controversies in which writers such as Joyce and others as well as himself were inevitably involved, and the official censorship which could ban books on religious and 'moral' grounds. As for O'Casey's failing to continue his Dublin realism, the germs of his later experimental surrealist and symbolic plays are present in his early work. O'Casey left Ireland a month after the Abbey riots, to receive the Hawthornden prize for *Juno and the Paycock*; in 1927 he married Eileen Reynolds Carey, a young Irish actress who had acted in the London production of *The Plough and the Stars*, and from then on lived permanently in England, eventually settling in 1938 in Devon, where he died in 1964.

## Career in exile

After the three Dublin plays, which had fixed him in the public mind as a writer of realistic plays about Dublin, O'Casey's next play, *The Silver Tassie* (1928), had an unexpected style and setting. It was about the British army in the First World War, its hero a soldier severely wounded in battle, who is paralysed and loses his girl to the comrade who has rescued him. Its most experimental feature was a surrealist second act, representing the fighting at the front. To O'Casey's surprise and bitter disappointment, this was rejected by the Abbey Theatre. Yeats objected to its experimentalism, and to its non-Irish subject. It seems unreasonable that he should have taken this view; he himself experimented with stylised, masked and 'chanted' drama. O'Casey was incensed at Yeats's suggestion that he was writing about something he did not know or care about and that he should keep to Irish themes. The cause and manner of his rejection estranged O'Casey from the Abbey Theatre; he was consequently deprived of a 'working' relationship with a theatre that would regularly stage his work. From now on his plays were mainly written for publication, and not for immediate production (though most were eventually staged either in England or in America). This detachment from a theatre has great disadvantages for any dramatist, to whom the rehearsal period is often crucial and productive. When O'Casey eventually saw his plays on the stage, he often made cuts and changes. The separation also harmed the Abbey Theatre itself, by cutting it off from one of its greatest dramatists, who was to write more adventurous, less parochial plays than it subsequently produced. It eventually staged *The Silver Tassie* in 1935; O'Casey and Yeats were reconciled, though he never resumed his close connections with the theatre. The play ran for a week and was considered 'immoral'.

The plays O'Casey wrote after breaking his connection with the Abbey Theatre include two one-act plays, *A Pound on Demand* (1932), a comedy in Irish dialect about two drunks in a Post Office, and *The End of the Beginning* (1937), a farce. But his eight major plays fall into two groups—four 'prophetic', propagandist plays, and four satirical fantasies.

The 'prophetic' plays dealt with current settings from the American Depression to the Second World War. *Within the Gates* (1933) takes place in a London park, with stylised characters representing contemporary 'types', and an 'Everywoman' heroine. O'Casey was in favour of real life and spontaneous joy, and not the false nostalgia of currently successful plays like Noel Coward's *Cavalcade* of 1931 ('Coward codology'). *The Star Turns Red* (1940) has a strike setting not unlike the 1913 Larkin strike; its hero, 'Red Jim', modelled on Larkin, represents the virtues of Communism in a symbolic war between Fascists and Communists. *Red Roses for Me* (1942) is set in Dublin during the 1913 strike and is close to O'Casey's own experience in the Labour movement. It includes nationalism, religious conflict, police charges and other 'real' Irish issues, but its climactic scene is a transformation of the Dublin quays into a place of joy, colour and light in a symbolic dance of life. *Oak Leaves and Lavender* (1946) is set in the Battle of Britain in the Second World War; it has semi-realistic scenes, with fantastic masques and stylised episodes, and ghosts as well as real characters.

O'Casey's four satirical fantasies have elements of farce, music-hall comedy, circus and concert. They all take place in rural Ireland. In *Purple Dust* (1945) two pompous Englishmen try to restore an Elizabethan mansion in an Irish village but are thwarted by comic Irish peasants and a great flood. In *Cock-a-Doodle-Dandy* (1949) the cock is a man-sized fantasy figure, a magician fighting for the forces of life and joy against Irish petty bureaucracy, Catholicism and capitalism. *The Bishop's Bonfire* (1955) is a melodramatic farce about preparations for the bishop's visit; it aroused a storm of opposition in Ireland for its 'anti-clericalism' even before it was staged at the Gaiety Theatre in 1955. Another controversy was caused by *The Drums of Father Ned* (1958), commissioned for the Dublin Tostal Festival; it was a burlesque about an Irish festival. The drums signify life, love and joy. The play was censured and censored, and O'Casey forbade all productions of his plays in Ireland henceforth (the ban lasted until 1964). A short collection of one-act satiric comedies published in 1961 containing *Figuro in the Night* (banned in London), *Behind the Green Curtains* and *The Moon Shines on Kylenamoe* completed O'Casey's dramatic output.

O'Casey's literary activity, however, was not confined to the theatre. His prose is exciting and provocative, often causing as much controversy as his plays, and much of it is banned in Ireland, including *Windfalls* (1934), a book of poems, short stories and one-act plays, and *The Green Crow* (1957). His short story 'I wanna woman' was censored by its English printer in 1933. Some of O'Casey's most trenchant opinions appeared in *The Flying Wasp* (1937), a collection of articles, essays and reviews, particularly on theatrical subjects. His criticism is perceptive, acid, witty and irreverent. But his prose can also be extraordinarily moving, like the account of his 21-year-old son's death in *Under a Colored Cap* ('Articles merry and mournful with comments and a song', 1963). The most sustained sequence of his prose is in his six autobiographies: *I Knock at the Door* (1939), *Pictures in the Hallway* (1942), *Drums Under the Window* (1946), *Inishfallen Fare Thee Well* (1949), *Rose and Crown* (1952), *Sunset and Evening Star* (1954). They are written in the third person, describing himself from without and within; they are full of compassion for the poor, contempt for the pompous, written in a varied, allusive style, ringing with wit, breaking from narrative into ballad, from stream of consciousness into scurrilous dialogue. They are a heightened revelation of himself and of Dublin, an illuminating background to his life, and masterly examples of autobiographical prose. It can be seen that certain themes run through his life and work: a lack of reverence for shibboleths, a belief in the forces of life and joy, and a rage against poverty and oppression.

# A note on the text

*Juno and the Paycock* first appeared at the Abbey Theatre Dublin on 3 March 1924. It was first published with *The Shadow of a Gunman* in *Two Plays*, Macmillan, London and New York, 1925. It was published alone as *Juno and the Paycock* in 'The Caravan Library', Macmillan, London, 1928. It next appeared in *Five Irish Plays* (by Sean O'Casey), Macmillan, London, 1935. It was published as *Juno and the Paycock. The Plough and The Stars*, ed. Guy Boas, in 'The Scholar's Library', Macmillan Education, London and Basingstoke, 1948; in *Collected Plays*, four volumes, (Macmillan, London and New York, 1949-51 (in Vol. I, 1949)); and in Saint Martin's Library in *Three Plays*, Macmillan, London, 1957, reprinted up to 1975—this is the edition used in these Notes.

# Part 2

# Summaries
*of* JUNO AND THE PAYCOCK

## A general summary

The play is set in a tenement house in Dublin, in the poor 'two-room tenancy' of the Boyle family. The date is 1922, during the civil war between those Irishmen who accept the Irish Free State Treaty with England, giving Ireland the status of a dominion within the British Commonwealth, and those 'die-hard' or entrenched Republicans who consider the Treaty a betrayal of their ideal of a completely independent Ireland. The civil war, as well as forming a general background to the play, gives rise to one of its four main plots, all of which are held together by the dominating figure of Juno Boyle. This plot concerning her son Johnny, who has been wounded in the two previous Republican conflicts of 1916 and 1920, provides most of the play's tension and suspense. The story of his betrayal of his Republican comrade and neighbour, Robbie Tancred, is unfolded by allusion, reaction and accusation through the play's three acts; retribution for having 'informed' draws closer and closer from the first mysterious knocks and strange visitors to the two 'Irregulars' or extreme Republicans who take him away to be shot at the end of Act III. This plot allows memorable moments like the funeral of Robbie Tancred, and Johnny's hysterical 'vision' of Tancred's dead body. Juno's part in it includes her maternal worry and grief for her son, and her view of the Civil War as wasteful, destructive, and irrelevant to the real problems of Irish life.

Another plot which involves Juno on several levels is that of the will. The Boyles are demonstrated throughout the first act to be extremely poor, living on credit and scarcely able to afford food. Only Juno is earning; her daughter Mary is on strike; Johnny has lost his arm so cannot work; her husband 'Captain Boyle' is an idler who cannot or will not find a job. At the beginning of Act I we see Juno despairing over money and despising her husband for strutting idly around like a 'paycock' (peacock) with his friend Joxer Daly. At the end of the act, Captain Boyle is told by Charlie Bentham, a schoolteacher turned lawyer, that he has been left 'anything between £1500 and £2000' in his cousin's will. The Boyles' life is changed to one of parties and plenty: Act II is full of the cheap luxuries which they buy for themselves on credit raised in expectation of their weath. Juno's attitude to Captain Boyle becomes more tolerant, and she too spends without her previous grinding worry about where the money is to come from. In Act III it is disclosed that the will was incompetently drawn up by Bentham; the Boyles are to get no money. Their creditors close in, their new possessions are taken away, and Juno's feeling for her husband reverts to scorn: he has known for some time that the will is invalid and has continued to live on credit.

A third plot concerns Juno's daughter Mary, seen first as an independent girl of intellectual ideas and Labour sympathies, reading Ibsen, going on strike, quoting trade union 'principles'. She is being courted by another Trade unionist, Jerry Devine, with whom she was once, but is no longer, in love. In Act II she has thrown Jerry over for Charlie Bentham; by Act III Bentham has gone away leaving her pregnant. Jerry then reappears to reaffirm his love for her until she tells him that she is going to have a baby, when he rejects her cruelly— 'Have you fallen as low as that?' Juno rallies to her daughter's defence when Captain Boyle turns against her; she decides to leave him to make a new home for Mary's baby—a positive, optimistic dedication of herself to the new generation.

A fourth plot, the backbone of the play, links these stories of Johnny, the will, and Mary: that of Mrs Boyle and her husband, or 'Juno and the Paycock'. Their relationship moves from antagonism born of poverty in the first act (with Joxer the outward and visible sign of Captain Boyle's fecklessness) to a temporary truce when they think they have money; by the end of the play Captain Boyle has failed his family and Juno renounces him: 'I've done all I could an' it was all no use—he'll be hopeless till the end of his days'. The Boyles' home is dead and empty; Johnny has been executed, the furniture has been taken away, and Captain Boyle is out getting drunk with Joxer, providing no support of any kind for his family. Juno and Mary leave, and in the play's tragically funny ending, Captain Boyle and Joxer stagger back to the tenement, full of bombast and drink, and without noticing that the flat is completely empty, decide that the world is in what to them is its usual 'terrible state o' chassis' or chaos.

Mary's and Johnny's stories are tragic; the will gives many opportunities for laughing at the newly 'rich' Boyles; Juno's exchanges with her husband can be bitter or amusing; the repartee between Captain Boyle and Joxer can be vicious or funny. The contrast between tragic and comic elements is one of O'Casey's principal methods of making his dramatic effects: Captain Boyle's fictitious heroic reminiscences make an ironic counterpoint to Johnny's secret treachery; Tancred's funeral is given powerful pathos by its juxtaposition with the Boyles' raucous party.

The four parallel plots draw attention to four major issues, some of Irish, some of wider interest, and all matters of deep concern to O'Casey. Johnny's republicanism relates to O'Casey's own early nationalist activities, to Irish nationalism in general, and to the gap between jingoistic nationalist principles and the true needs of the Irish poor. The invalid will illustrates the desperate joylessness of the poor that only money can overcome—O'Casey always saw poverty as robbing its victims of dignity and joy. Mary's trade unionism is connected with O'Casey's admiration for Jim Larkin, and with his commitment to the world Labour movement. Juno's development from a grumbling, harassed drudge to a figure of strength and nobility moving decisively away from the dead past to help the new generation, echoes a theme expressed by dramatists such as Ibsen and Shaw: the necessity of finding one's identity and of liberating oneself from deadening convention into life.

# Detailed summaries

## Act I

In this act the major characters are introduced, often with detailed stage instructions. As well as giving realistic descriptions of the set, these can cover the characters' external features (Captain Boyle is 'stout, grey-haired and stocky. His neck is short, and his head looks like a stone ball that one sometimes sees on top of a gate-post'), or their internal make-up (Jerry is 'a type, becoming very common now in the Labour movement, of a mind knowing enough to make the mass of his associates, who know less, a power, and too little to broaden that power for the benefit of all'). They can compare the characters as they are and as they might have been (Juno has a look of 'listless monotony and harassed anxiety, blending with an expression of mechanical resistance. Were circumstances favourable, she would probably be a handsome, active and clever woman') or give even more complex insights (Mary has two forces in her mind—'one, through the circumstances of her life, pulling her back; the other, through the influence of books she has read, pushing her forward').

The stage directions describe a poor slum dwelling. Mary reads from a newspaper the gruesome death-wounds of the victim of an ambush, to which Johnny reacts violently; as Mary says, 'he's gettin' very sensitive, all of a sudden'. Juno mentions that the victim was a Diehard with whom Johnny was once connected. She also prepares us before her husband Captain Boyle comes 'sailin' in with the boul' Joxer': he is out of work, has exhausted the health insurance and unemployment benefit; he is 'constantly singing'. Mary too is a source of grievance to Juno; she is full of trade union jargon: 'The hour is past now when we'll ask the employer's permission', or 'a principle's a principle'. Juno takes a short term view of the trade unions as causing a hundred to be out of work instead of one; she sees life in terms of immediate credit or debt. It is Juno who reveals a different Johnny from the one we see on stage, fearful, jumpy, dependent for protection on a holy picture and a votive light—the 'light lightin' before the picture of the Virgin'. She sees him as the boy hero who got 'a bullet in the hip' in the Easter Rising of 1916 when Irish rebels held the Post Office against the British and declared a Republic, and whose arm was shattered by a bomb in O'Connell Street in Dublin during the period when the 'Black and Tans' were in operation in Ireland.

Jerry Devine brings action into this exposition—the priest has found a job for Captain Boyle; Juno sends him to look for her husband in the pub and waits in hiding for the Captain's return. The comic business which follows shows Captain Boyle and Joxer in full flow of rhetoric, the Captain foraging for food and Joxer sponging from him. They complain about Juno's grumbling and work out a scheme for evading work; their conversation is larded with rhetoric, fairy tales, songs, repetitions. This is pure comedy, but Juno's words when she shows herself are barbed, ironic, and not wholly funny: she taunts Captain Boyle with 'not able to lift your arms with the pains in your legs', 'your poor wife slavin' to keep the bit in your mouth, an' you gallivantin' about all the day like a paycock!' She reveals the essential lie in his whole personality and name: 'everybody callin' you "Captain" an' you only wanst on the wather, in an oul' collier from here to Liverpool'. They bicker about his drinking and he swears that for the last three weeks he has not tasted 'a dhrop of intoxicatin' liquor'. With much circumstantial detail, he pretends that he and Joxer are on the point of getting a job, but reveals his true horror of work when Jerry returns with news of the priest's job—'How d'ye expect me to go up a ladder with these legs?' Although Juno still perfunctorily performs the duties of a wife ('You'll sit down an' take your breakfast'), her scornful attitude to him has been established, and her determination to 'stay an' hunt that Joxer' matches her stance that it is Joxer who is leading Captain Boyle astray: 'Oh, you'll do a lot o' good as long as you continue to be a butty o' Joxer's.'.

Jerry and Mary, left alone, discuss their past and their future: they have once been in love; he wants to marry her if he is elected to the secretaryship of their trade union with a salary. He speaks in a mixture of lyricism and aggression, swearing 'No matther what happens, you'll always be the same to me'. She is hostile, and always has what he calls 'the bitther word' for him—'you'll make me hate you'. He accuses her of having somebody else—'a thin lanky strip of a Micky Dazzler' and creates such a 'hillabaloo' that Captain Boyle arrives to object. Jerry demands to kiss Mary's 'little, tiny, white hand'; such disrespect ('nice goin's on in front of her father') and Jerry's answer to his objection—'Ah, dhry up'—outrage Boyle, who for the first time in the play produces his immortal, portentous and unprofound maxim 'the whole worl's in a state o' chassis'.

As the Captain cooks his breakfast sausage, the first of a series of intruders arrives—a sewing machine salesman; another knock brings Joxer who refuses to look out in case he is shot; Boyle sees 'a fella in a thrench coat'. The 'bullet in the kisser' that Joxer dreads, and Captain Boyle's fear that if Juno comes in she will catch them 'like rats in a thrap', economically give an idea of the general atmosphere of war in which the characters live; their conversation is loaded with military and political imagery.

Captain Boyle's conversations with Joxer, although apparently comic, establish the poverty of his intellectual, moral and spiritual outlook, as bleak as their poor home. Mary's reading of Ibsen is 'thrash'; Jerry Devine is unmanly 'I never heard him usin' a curse; I don't believe he was ever dhrunk in his life—sure he's not like a Christian at all'; the Roman Catholic clergy have too much power over the people, have treated them badly and betrayed their leaders; they want their flock to be 'livin' in the Chapel' and insist on 'work, work, work for me an' you'. Captain Boyle's nationalism is insincere jingoism, and a desire to profit from Johnny's 'heroism': 'it's a curious way to reward Johnny be makin' his poor oul' father work'. Joxer agrees with Captain Boyle in all things ('You're afther takin the word out o' me mouth'); and eggs him on to the full flood of his seafaring ·memories. He echoes another of the Captain's unprofound philosophical musings: 'I ofen looked up at the sky an' assed meself the question—what is the stars, what is the stars?' followed by 'what is the moon?'. He urges him to rebel against Juno—'It's time you showed a little spunk'; but has to fly out of the window onto the roof when she comes back.

She heralds 'the news that'll give you the chance o' your life'; he is to change his trousers for the arrival of Charlie Bentham to whom she defers and apologises—'that man o' mine always make a litther o' the' place'. Juno introduces Johnny to Bentham with a potted history of his wounds—'none can deny he done his bit for Irelan" and the bitter qualification 'if that's goin' to do him any good'. Johnny is as full of Republican principles as Mary is of Labour ones. 'Ireland only half free'll never be at peace while she has a son left to pull a trigger'—for him too 'a principle's a principle'.

Bentham in this act is not openly connected with Mary: he is the agent for revealing the will. He reads it out in full and explains that it will be between £1500 and £2000. The will is the first definite incident in the play—up to now the scenes have been being set, the characters established. Much of what has been explained has been set in the past—Johnny's heroism, Jerry's and Mary's love affair, the longstanding antagonism of Juno's marriage. Now word from outside brings something new to adjust to: the Boyles' reactions set up a new pattern in the family. Mary's is simple and enthusiastic: 'A fortune, father, a fortune!' Johnny sees the money as an escape route: 'we'll be able to get out o' this place now'. Juno sees it, surprisingly, as a liberation for Captain Boyle: 'You won't have to trouble about a job for awhile, Jack'. His reactions are more complex; first he assumes the role of business man: 'An' how much'll be comin' out of it?'; next he offers Bentham a drink: 'A wet—a jar—a boul!' He renounces Joxer (who is still on the roof, within earshot:) 'Juno, I'm done with Joxer'. Joxer jumps in through the window and in his turn betrays Captain Boyle's pretences—'I have to laugh every time I look at the deep-sea sailor; an' a row on the river ud make him sea-sick!' He scornfully accuses him of 'lookin' for work, an' prayin' to God he won't get it!' Captain Boyle is going to be 'a new man from this out'; they will keep themselves to themselves. He sings 'O me darlin' Juno, I will be thrue to thee', a second-hand echo of 'O me darlin' Jenny . . . ' that raises our doubts about the permanence of the rift between the two friends.

The relationships between the characters have by now been established, unchanged through Act I except for the switch between Juno and Joxer in Captain Boyle's loyalties at the end. Juno is the central figure in this act: to Johnny she is a protective mother. She is proud of his past yet bitter that he has lost his manhood in his fighting—for to her the right to work is the working man's best principle. To Mary she is a practical, grumbling, critical mother. Between Juno and the Captain is a long-dead marriage; disillusion on her part and fear on his have eroded whatever life they once had together. So far, all the relationships and links in the play ray out from her except for Mary's with Jerry and Captain Boyle's with Joxer. Her own feeling for Joxer is close to hatred. It is not just his drinking and idling, but his continual presence that annoys her. Captain Boyle has only to call and Joxer comes downstairs at the ready. The setting of the play within the tenement magnifies every emotion: they are prey to every salesman and neighbour, and have no privacy. Johnny's nerves are put even further on edge by the neighbour directly above him trampling like a horse over his head; Captain Boyle cannot even change his trousers without driving Johnny 'mad', nor can Jerry propose to Mary without Captain Boyle in his turn being disturbed by the 'hillabaloo'. Mary is 'degraded by her environment'; it has given Juno her 'look of listless monotony and harassed anxiety'.

By the end of Act I, O'Casey has set up four special areas of tension for his four plots. Two have merely been stated: Johnny's fear about the ambush, set in the general atmosphere of war, and Mary's two forces—her circumstances pulling her back and the books she has read pushing her forward. Two others have been stated and appear to have been resolved: the will has suddenly enabled the forces of poverty to be overcome by money, and in the Juno-Captain Boyle plot, the struggle between Juno and Joxer for the Captain's loyalities has apparently been resolved in favour of Juno.

NOTES AND GLOSSARY

*Title:* In classical mythology Juno was the only 'married' wife of Jupiter the king of the Gods. She was the patroness of marriage and childbirth, and had great power. She had many disputes with Jupiter, and was extremely jealous of him. All of these factors are relevant to the Juno of the play. The peacock was her bird; the 'eyes' in its tail represent the hundred eyes of Argus her messenger. Here, the 'paycock' or peacock is also associated with the jay in the fable who decked itself out in peacock's feathers.

**A picture of the Virgin...a floating votive light:** The worship of the Virgin Mary, the mother of Christ, was particularly developed in Irish Roman Catholics. The votive light represented an offering to her, often in fulfilment of a vow, and also sanctuary

**beyant:** beyond

**paycock:** peacock

**Diehard:** entrenched extreme Republican, one of those opposed to the signing of the Free State Treaty

**boul':** bold (ironically used for 'fine')

**what a good Samaritan he is!:** Ironically used for 'how charitable he is'—the Good Samaritan in the Bible (Gospel according to Saint Luke 10:33) showed generosity to a man who had been robbed

**health insurance:** a scheme by which one paid small sums each week so that compensation would be paid if one were too ill to work

**unemployment dole:** payment by the State to those out of work

**A Novena:** A popular devotion paid to Saint Anthony of Padua on the first Fridays of nine consecutive months

**Easter Week:** in the Easter Rising of 1916.

**the fight in O'Connell Street:** during the Black and Tan War of 1920

**wan:** one

**snug:** intimate room in a public house (an inn or tavern)

**Sweet Spirit, hear me prayer!:** part of an aria about the spell of music from *Lurline*, an opera by W.V. Wallace about the Lorelei myth of the Rhine nymph. The first of many such operatic airs in the play, often in ironic contrast to the singer or the context: 'The past forgive, the future spare,/Great spirit hear my pray'r./Oh! leave me not alone in grief/Send this blighted heart relief/Make thou my life thy future care/Great spirit hear my prayer'; with the refrain 'hear, oh, hear' as Captain Boyle sings it. He was in fact to be left 'alone' by the end of the play

**affeydavey:** affidavit, a written statement on oath

**Deidre of the Sorras:** Deirdre of the Sorrows, a heroine of Celtic myth whose beauty was foretold to be fatal. Conchubhar King of Ulster kept her from childhood to be his wife but she eloped with Naoise, one of three Sons of Usna. Conchubhar killed the three brothers and Deirdre committed suicide. The legend was very popular with Abbey playwrights—AE (George Russell) wrote a play about in it 1901, Yeats did so in 1906 and Synge's *Deirdre of the Sorrows* was not completed when he died in 1909.

**grousin':** grumbling

**ofen:** often

**the cup that cheers but doesn't . . . :** misquotation from the poet William Cowper's praise of tea, 'the cups,/That cheer but not inebriate'

**butty:** friend

**on the blow o' dinner, the blow up for dinner:** the foreman blows his whistle for the men to stop work at dinner-time

**lashin's o':** lots of

**moleskins:** working trousers made of mole-skin

**long-tailed shovel, navvy:** labourers' spades

**for want of a nail the shoe was lost . . . :** a progressive proverb by the end of which the battle is lost 'all through the loss of a horse-shoe nail'

**gallivantin':** gadding about

**Christo For Columbus:** the Irish for 'Christopher' is 'Criostofoir', pronounced roughly 'Christo For'

**yous:** dialect 'you'

**knock out:** find

**pereeogative:** his own mispronunciation of 'prerogative'

**me bucko:** Irish slang from 'my buck' or 'my dandy'

**a wake:** an Irish funeral celebration

**clicked with:** suddenly fallen in love with

**chiselurs:** children

**chassis:** his own mispronunciation of chaos

**When the Robins nest agen [again]:** an American ballad by F. Howard, of a girl waiting for her lover to come home, though she fears 'his proud ship' is 'wreck'd at sea'

**in the kisser:** in the face

*The [A] Doll's House, Ghosts, an' The Wild Duck:* plays by Henrik Ibsen (1828–1906) published respectively in 1879, 1881 and 1884; each seriously questions some social convention by showing characters trapped in their marriages or families, from which they must free themselves by finding their true identities.

*Elizabeth, or Th'Exile o' Sibayria: Elizabeth, or the Exiles of Siberia* was a popular moral tale about filial piety by Madam Sophie Cottin (Marie Risteau, 1770-1807); Elizabeth walked 2,000 miles to ask the Czar to release her father from exile in Siberia

**argufy:** argue

**Virol:** an easily digested patent strengthening food

**the people in '47:** He is referring to the Irish famine of 1845-47, when the potato crop failed and the people starved. Although there was corn, it was for export

**Parnell:** Charles Stewart Parnell (1846-1891), leader of the Parliamentary Party in the fight for Home Rule, who was brought down (partly by the Church) after the scandal of his affair with Mrs Kitty O'Shea involving her divorce

**The Fenians:** the secret revolutionary society formed in 1857 to overthrow British rule in Ireland

| | |
|---|---|
| **mulin':** | here, working like mules |
| **craw-thumpin':** | breast-beating; the prayer 'Sacred Heart of Jesus have mercy on us' was repeated three times, and the breast beaten each time |
| **Confraternity:** | a religious group devoted to the worship of the Sacred Heart. Devotion to the 'Sacred Heart of Jesus' is often alluded to in the play: one type of religious picture showed Christ with his bleeding heart revealed on his chest |
| **have it out:** | settle a dispute |

**How can a man die better:** a misquotation from *Horatius* by Macaulay (1800-59), highly comic in the context of facing Juno. Horatius held Rome against the Etruscans in the year 360BC by keeping a bridge: 'Then out spake brave Horatius,/the Captain of the Gate:/'To every man upon this earth/Death cometh soon or late./And how can man die better/Than facing fearful odds,/For the ashes of his fathers,/And the temples of his Gods'.

| | |
|---|---|
| **Boy Scout:** | one of the Fianna, the junior branch of the Irish Republican Army |

**Ireland only half free'll never be at peace:** an adaptation of the Sinn Fein motto 'Ireland unfree will never be at peace'; the Republicans considered the Free State with its limited self-rule and exclusion of Ulster to be only half independent

**prognosticator and procrastinator:** meaningless combination of similar words to sound insulting

| | |
|---|---|
| **Sorra many:** | not many |

**St. Vincent de Paul Society:** a religious charitable institution

**A wet-a jar-a boul!:** all slang words for a drink

**Guh sayeree jeea ayera:** phonetic transcription of the Irish 'Go saoiridh Dia Eire', 'God save Ireland'.

| | |
|---|---|
| **a slate off:** | a slate off one's roof or something wrong with one's head, that is, mad |
| **aw rewaeawr:** | au revoir |

---

## Act II

---

Two days after Captain Boyle's rejection of Joxer we find them together again—but although Captain Boyle may not have 'done with Joxer', he is 'a new man' in many ways. He takes a superior view of money, handling large cheques, from 'a couple o' hundred' to three pounds five shillings of which he can hand Joxer the five shillings. Their relationship is different now; paradoxically, Joxer is more outspoken than in the days when both were poor—perhaps because of Captain Boyle's rejection of him. He comes out with his own views first, instead of merely echoing Boyle, from whom he now often differs. They sum up what has been happening—the Boyles have been buying furniture on credit; the Captain has been congratulated by the priest; Mary has finished with Jerry and it looks as if she will marry Bentham. Discussing the priest, Captain Boyle turns right around from his earlier views. Now he does not like anyone to 'talk disrespectful of Father Farrell': it is 'very near to blasfeemey', and the priests have always been 'in the van of the fight for Irelan's freedom'. Joxer still holds their old anti-clerical views. He thinks Bentham 'a darlin' man', which irritates Captain Boyle ('What's darlin' about him?'); he suggests that Mary's two suitors are direct opposites of each other: 'Jerry believin' in nothin', an' Bentham believin' in everythin' '; Jerry the Labourite 'says all is man an' no God' whereas Bentham the Theosophist 'says all is God an' no man'.

Boyle asks him to a party later—'a quiet jar an' a song or two'. This, the first time that we see Joxer as an invited guest, is a measure of Captain Boyle's easier relationship with Juno. She now appears with Mary, carrying a gramophone that she has bought; she is amiable with everyone and disappointed that Johnny is not interested in her gramophone. He is morose, sullen, repetitive: he has been sleeping each night with a different relative—'I can rest nowhere, nowhere, nowhere'. Bentham arrives, still the object of many deferential attentions from Juno. Captain Boyle treats him as an equal now that he can discuss the stock market with him: 'Consols was down half per cent. That's serious, min' you, an' shows the whole country's in a state o' chassis'. The conversation leads by way of religion to Theosophy, the study of psychic and spiritual phenomena which was then current in Dublin—W.B. Yeats and A.E. (George Russell) were among the well-known Theosophists of the day. Bentham expatiates on it, from its 'one Universal Life-Breath' to its 'scientific' explanation of ghosts: that the release of psychic energy at the scene of 'sensational actions' enables a person connected with them to see 'the whole affair'.

His words tap a nerve of superstition going back much further than 'scientific theory': they cause a violent reaction—or over-reaction—in Johnny. When he rushes into the inner room, screams and rushes back onto the stage, he changes the whole nature of the play. Now we are sure that he is involved in something terrifying; his taciturnity becomes a flood of praying, pleading words; he calls on God, on his family, and particularly on Juno. His alteration now casts her in a different role. Whereas she has up to now been a sharp-tongued wife, a mildly protective or nagging Mother, an ordinary, poor, occasionally vulgar woman with an expressly non-heroic part, she is now equated with the Virgin Mary by a direct echo. Johnny calls on the Virgin: 'Blessed Mother o' God, shelter me, shelther your son!', and then on his real mother: 'Sit here, sit here, mother . . . between me an' the door'. This is the first of several intimations of Juno as the Blessed Virgin.

When Johnny explains what he has 'seen'—'Robbie Tancred kneelin' down before the statue . . . an' the red light shinin' on him . . . he turned an' looked at me . . . an' I seen the woun's bleedin' in his breast'—we remember the newspaper report at the beginning of Act I which described the body with seven wounds, one 'in the left breast penethratin' the heart'. The reactions to Johnny's outburst are polarised into male and female. Juno's quick 'what ails you?' and immediate small comforts of whiskey, quilt and bed are echoed by Mary's 'Johnny, Johnny, what ails you?' Captain Boyle and Bentham on the other hand are phlegmatically reasonable: for Captain Boyle 'it was only a shadda', for Bentham 'it was simply due to an overwrought imagination', to which he adds the bland and unconvincing reassurance 'we all get that way at times'. When Johnny asks 'Oh, why did he look at me like that?', Juno's consolation that 'it was only in his own head it was' is ironical to the audience though not to the Boyles; we feel that Johnny is indeed carrying his guilt in his head. He is now implicated in Tancred's death: the statue is no longer a symbol of protection and light but one of vengeance, death and blood. The atmosphere of the play becomes one of melodrama and gloom. When Bentham goes in to check the statue (that alarming task having been passed from Juno to Captain Boyle to Mary to him), he reports that the light is 'burning bravely', and that everything is 'just as it was', but everything is not now really as it was. Up to now we have seen only comedy; even the reports of Tancred's death have been hearsay. From now on tragedy is inherent in the play.

But no sooner has tragedy been established than comedy reasserts itself—a knock, and instead of any sinister retributory figure, Joxer and Maisie Madigan arrive for the party; they make an anticlimax after the emotions of Johnny's hysterics. The tension is lightened but only artificially, by drink, songs, trivial anecdotes and reminiscences. Mrs Madigan's stories are of summer, the country, youth, dancing and singing. Even in her memories, politics and revolution form the background to her songs; while she was singing 'You'll Remember Me', the Black and Tans were brutally 'Jazz dancin''.

This sing-song is central to the play in a literal and a literary sense. The songs that are sung are not to do with Ireland's troubles, nor with the real life that is going on outside, nor even ballads of the recent past: they are romantic and escapist, culled from opera or operetta via the drawing-rooms of richer people. The only Irish song that is heard here is one of the *Irish Melodies* of Thomas Moore (1779-1852). It is one of Joxer's 'shut-eyed wans', that he would sing with great feeling if he could; but he cannot remember it, nor any of the others he tries. Johnny, nerves grating as usual, asks for the gramophone, the epitome of cheap music and worthless luxury, to 'stop Joxer's bawlin''.

Again the plays shifts from comedy to tragedy with Mrs Tancred's appearance on her way to her son's funeral. The contrast of her grief and the party jollity is simple and strong. She is a completely tragic character, who removes the effects of the civil war from abstract 'principle' to human value. To her Tancred's death is not a newspaper report or a statistic—to her he had 'a darlin' head'; in contrast with Joxer's cheap catchphrase, hers is a tender, lyrical 'darlin''. Her elegy is a mixture of prayerbook phrases, personal sorrow and traditional Irish keening (or formal wailing) for the dead. We must remember that a Roman Catholic dreads above all dying unattended by a priest. When Mrs Tancred describes her son 'lyin' for a whole night stretched out on the side of a lonely country lane' she is horrified not only by the loneliness of his death but by the absence of the last rites to provide religious solace and entry into heaven. This gives special poignancy to her call to the the mother of Christ, traditionally the intercessor for man with her son: 'O Blessed Virgin, where were you when me darlin' son was riddled with bullets?' She also gives us new information: her son was not only a victim, but a murderer himself—he was 'the leadher of the ambush where me nex' door neighbour, Mrs Mannin', lost her Free State soldier son'. She equates 'the two of us oul' women, standin' one on each side of a scales o' sorra, balanced by the bodies of our two dead darlin' sons', and makes her humanitarian prayer, based on the Roman Catholic prayerbook, and soon to be echoed by Juno, 'Sacred Heart of the crucified Jesus, take away our hearts o' stone . . . an' give us hearts o' flesh! . . . Take away this murdherin' hate . . . an' give us Thine own eternal love!' It is noticeable that none of the Boyles pays any tribute to Mrs Tancred's son as the other neighbours do ('the Republic won't be always down . . . he died à noble death'). They offer only the small physical comforts of tea, a shawl, advice to stay at home.

The mood of the play changes again when Mrs Tancred leaves, and we hear the Boyles' first (and only) open discussion of the civil war. Juno considers it 'going to Hell' to be a Diehard like Tancred 'with his

Republic first, an' Republic last, an' Republic over all'. Bentham thinks 'the only way to deal with a mad dog is to destroy him'; Captain Boyle that 'we've nothin' to do with these things ... that's the Government's business ... they don't affect us', a view we now know to be ironically far from the truth since his own son is directly involved. Johnny's only reaction is to disown Tancred: 'he was no friend o' mine. I never cared for him, an' he could never stick me. It's not because he was Commandant of the Battalion that I was Quarther-Masther of, that we were friends'. Juno's immediate reaction is expository—to explain to Bentham who Mrs Tancred is—the tenant of 'the two-pair back'. Through Juno the extent and the closeness of the civil war is made clear to us for the first time. She tells us that Mrs Tancred has allowed the Republicans to use her rooms, so that the tenement has been raided by special police looking for arms. Now three of the families in the tenement have lost sons. Juno develops three major points: first, that no matter what military side he was on, Robbie was Mrs Tancred's 'poor son'; then, that the civil war is their business ('Sure, if it's not our business, I don't know whose business it is'); and that people like Mrs Tancred, by collaborating, are allowing it to infiltrate into their very house.

The Boyles resume their party, but this time it is shown in counterpoint to Tancred's funeral, which passes in the street. Captain Boyle recites his own poem which contains all the clichés of easy-going Irishness: it contains a best friend, hating the Boss, lying in jail, not going to church, and always with a penny for a friend. As the gramophone plays a ballad of the cheapest stage Irish 'togetherness', 'If you're Irish, come into the parlour', Needle Nugent the tailor comes into their parlour, outraged, to demand silence for the funeral. He expresses not sympathy for Mrs Tancred but sentimental jingoism—'Have none of yous any respect for the Irish people's National regard for the dead?' Maisie Madigan accuses him of hypocrisy—he is an opportunist who goes to Republican funerals by day and spends the night making uniforms for the new Free State police, the Civic Guard. Juno sees in him a different form of Irish hypocrisy—that of paying respect to the dead and neglecting the living. This is a theme dear to O'Casey, and one of the reasons that he preferred the Labour movement to the nationalist one; the strong Irish cult of the dead hero did nothing to help the poor. It is illustrated by the number of wreaths on Tancred's coffin—someone has been able to afford for him in death a show he never had in life. The funeral hymn to the Sacred Heart is heard, a gloomy parallel with the party ballads; a funeral, like a party, is a source of excitement in dull slum life, so the family goes off to watch it—'a darlin' funeral'.

Now, at last, a young man enters—this time unheralded, a soft surprise compared with the previous false alarms. He is the reality: a Mobilizer from his Battalion, come to summon Johnny to account. He looks at Johnny for a moment and says 'Quarther-Masther Boyle'. Johnny is no longer Juno's lad or a hysterical cripple; he is Quartermaster Boyle, responsible for his actions. Our suspicion that he has been the cause of Tancred's death is confirmed; he has informed against his comrade in arms, breaking his Republican oath. He finds a last remnant of spirit—'I won't go! . . . Haven't I done enough for Ireland?' The Mobilizer's 'No man can do enough for Ireland' sums up the sacrificial nature of Irish republicanism; the funeral in the background shows its consequences. The funeral prayer is heard outside to ironic effect; it is the Hail Mary, a prayer to the Virgin—Mary who has failed to be there when needed by Tancred; Mary who is a little like Juno, ready with small comforts and cups of tea but unable to protect against the realities of death and civil war.

In this act the focal figure is Johnny. His jumpiness makes him central by his over-reaction to everyone's words, from Bentham's scientific theory to Joxer's songs. He is directly linked now with Tancred's death; with the Mobilizer, representing the republican army; with Mary, who has developed a protective attitude to him, and with Juno, who is closely maternal. Captain Boyle is neutral, as detached from him as he is from everybody else. Comedy and tragedy are built up in turns, helped by a new comic character, Maisie Madigan, and a new tragic one, Mrs Tancred. Maisie Madigan is a parallel with Juno's frivolous side. Mrs Tancred, who is later to be the parallel with Juno's patriot's-mother side, is shown here in contrast with her; Juno is surrounded by her family and new possessions, while Mrs Tancred has nothing: 'Me home is gone now; he was me only child'. Bentham, scarcely present in Act I, is here one of the outsiders introduced to show new aspects of the Boyle family. Juno and even Mary are still deferential to him. His views on religion and politics draw forth the Boyles' opinions; his remarks on ghostly apparitions stimulate Johnny's hallucination.

Money too is a catalyst: as well as providing the Boyles with material objects it has changed their relationships with each other. Juno and Captain Boyle are no longer at loggerheads—she is less scornful, he more self-confident, with his 'dockyments', stocks and shares. A new dimension of possible truth, slimly based on his 'fortune', is added to his boasting; after all it is he who has brought the money into the family; he is now a bread-winner, if not a worker. He is not, however, 'a new man', and Joxer is back on the scene again. Captain Boyle and

Juno have something in common in this act—the urge to spend money; but we notice an essential difference in their reactions to the civil war—his detached, hers concerned. The realities of war have come closer, in the information we have received, in Tancred's funeral, and in Johnny's summons. In this act the four major plots develop along different lines. Johnny's jumpiness has turned to hysteria; we know that he has caused Tancred's death and that retribution for it is drawing closer. Mary is apparently settled with Bentham. The will is not in doubt; it has made the Boyles more open-handed and light-hearted. For June and Captain Boyle, hostilities have ceased.

NOTES AND GLOSSARY

**attackey case:** attaché case

**riz:** raised

**differ:** difference

**like the two Musketeers:** a joking comparison with the Three Musketeers in *The Three Musketeers* (1844) a novel by Dumas (1802–70); their motto was 'One for all and all for one'

**I met with Napper Tandy:** Napper Tandy (1740–1803) whose name is closely linked with the idea of exile. He fled to America in 1793, and thence to France where he was made a general. He landed in the north of Ireland in 1798, was later sentenced to death by the British but was extradited to France where he died. The ballad's most famous verse is 'I met with Napper Tandy and he took me by the hand;/ And says he, How's poor old Ireland, and how does she stand? /She's the most distressful country that ever yet has been,/ For they're hanging men and women too for wearin' o' the green'

**blasfeemey:** blasphemy

**the heart o' the rowl:** one of the best ('rowl' meaning a roll of tobacco, with the best and moistest tobacco at the centre or heart)

**bummer:** an idle, worthless person

**folleyin' you like a Guardian Angel:** following closely; the Angel who accompanied and protected one was a popular theme for hymns and sermons

**from this out:** from now on

**in the van:** in the forefront of battle

**Soggart Aroon:** ironically based on a ballad by Michael Scanlon (1836–1917) called 'Soggart Achree' (in Irish 'Soggart Aroon' and 'Soggart Achree' both mean 'Dear Priest'), suggesting that the priests hindered rather than helped the fight for Ireland's freedom

**gawkin':** staring

**the Story o' Irelan' ... Be J.L. Sullivan:** his confusion of J.L. Sullivan the boxer (1858–1918) and Alexander Martin Sullivan (1830–84) who wrote *The Story of Ireland*

**Boney's oraculum:** a cheap 'oracle' book named after Napoleon Buonaparte (1769–1821), with fortune-telling, cards and dreams

**he's wrong shipped:** he has the wrong idea

**kilt:** killed

**ower:** out of

**allanna:** endearment, from Irish 'a leanbh', my child

**Consols:** Consolidated shares on the stock market

**A theosophist:** one who believed in the 'wisdom-religion' propagated by the Theosophical Society or 'Universal Brotherhood' founded in 1875 by H.P. Blavatsky and others. Its members studied psychic and spiritual phenomena; its objects were: the Brotherhood of Man; the study of ancient world-religions; the development of man's latent divine powers. AE and Yeats were both follows of Madame Blavatsky, and there were several Irish Theosophist Lodges

**The Vedas:** four collections of ancient sacred Hindu literature, each divided into Mantra (hymns) and Brahmana (precepts), Aranyakas, (theology) and Upanishads (philosophy)

**Prawna:** the Prana, Sanskrit for 'breath', signifying the 'vital air' or 'life principle' in mystic and occult philosophy

**Yogi:** practiser of Yoga, Sanskrit for 'union', or the development of man's latent powers for achieving union with the Divine Spirit, by eight stages, each separating him further from material life and leading towards a state of enlightenment

**Charlie Chaplin an' Tommy Mix:** film stars, Charles Chaplin (1888–1977) a comedian, Tom Mix (1880–1940) a 'cowboy'

**puff:** life (puff of breath)

**a skelpin':** a smack

**Past Chief Ranger of the Dear Little Shamrock Branch of the Irish National Foresters:** an actual, flamboyantly green-uniformed society—a comment on the number of armies and groups militant in Ireland at the time

**kem:** came

**ball o' malt:** glass of whisky

**Gawn:** go on

**Home to our mountains:** a popular aria from the opera *Il Trovatore* (1853) by Verdi (1813–1901). The Troubadour soothes his mother to sleep after she has seen frightful visions—the exact reverse of Johnny and Juno. 'Home to our mountains, /Let us return love,/There in thy young days/ Peace had its reign./ There shall thy sweet song/ Fall on my slumbers/ There shall thy lute/ Make me joyous again. /Rest thee my mother; /Kneeling beside thee/ I will pour forth my troubadour lay./ O sing and wake now/ Thy sweet lute's soft numbers/ Lull me to rest, /Charm my sorrows away'

**If I were a blackbird . . . :** a slightly inaccurate rendering of a Dublin street ballad of the 1920s, whose last line is 'And I'd pillow my head on his lily white breast'

**green, white and orange:** the colours of the Republic flag

**when the Tans started their Jazz dancin':** when the Black and Tans started their atrocities

**An' you'll remember me:** from the opera *The Bohemian Girl* (1843) with words by Alfred Bunn (1796–1860), and music by M.W. Balfe (1808–70). 'When other lips and other hearts /Their tales of love shall tell,/ In language whose excess imparts /The power they feel so well,/ There may perhaps in such a scene, /Some recollections be,/ Of days that have as happy been,/ And you'll remember me, and you'll remember, you'll remember me'. Again the subject of the song is in contrast with the present time and with the revolutionary times in which Maisie sang it

**She is far from the lan':** a lyric from Thomas Moore's *Irish Melodies* (1808), about Sarah Curran the fiancée of Robert Emmet, the Irish Patriot who led an unsuccessful rebellion in 1803 and was hanged. It continues: 'But coldly she turns from their gaze, and weeps/ For her heart in his grave is lying'.

**I have heard the mavis singin':** from a romantic ballad 'Mary of Argyle', by Sydney Nelson (1800–62) writer of dramatic and regional songs

**collandher:** colander or sieve

**Tancred:** Tancred was a Christian hero of the Crusades in the opera of that name by Gioachino Rossini (1792–1868) the Italian composer

**'Let me like a soldier fall':** partial quotation from a song in *Maritana*, an English opera (1845) by Edward Fitzball (1792–1873) a prolific librettist, and W.V. Wallace (1812–69) an opera composer born in Ireland who worked in Australia, England and Germany. *Maritana* was very successful and was followed by *Lurline* (1849), an equally successful opera

**C.I.D.:** Criminal Investigation Department, the police detective force

**Civic Guards:** the new Irish Free State police force

**'If you're Irish come into the parlour':** a cheap ballad of false Irishness at its worst; 'If you're Irish, come into the parlour,/There's a welcome there for you./If your name is Timothy or Pat,/So long as you come from Ireland,/There's a welcome on the mat ... whoever you are, you're one of us/If you're Irish, this is the place for you'. It is a grotesque song in the context of civil war between Irishmen.

**To Jesus' Heart all burning:** a popular hymn to the Sacred Heart

**the Pillar:** A column surmounted by a statue of Horatio, Lord Nelson (1758–1805), the famous naval commander who was victor at the Battle of Trafalgar. It was in O'Connell Street, Dublin, but blown up in 1966

**gave the bend:** informed

**your oath:** as a member of the Irish Republican Brotherhood he would have sworn to 'do my utmost to establish the national independence of Ireland, and that I will bear true allegiance to the Supreme Council of the Irish Republic Brotherhood and Government of the Irish Republic and implicitly obey the Constitution of the Irish Republican Brotherhood and all my superior officers and that I will preserve inviolable the secrets of the organisation'. Johnny has thus failed to keep the oath of secrecy and is now refusing to obey his superior officers.

## Act III

We learn in the first line of Act III, which takes place two months after Act II, that Bentham has left Mary; this is the first of many disappointments for the Boyles. The relationships in this act are all of negation, rejection, loss and distance except for one solid, forward-looking bond forged between Juno and Mary. They open the act; Juno, so often the expositor of exact dates and events in the play, lets us know that Bentham has written 'not one line for the past month' to Mary. She is weary and ill, far from the independent girl of the first act, full of spirit and principles. We do not yet understand why Bentham has left her—for Mary it is because the Boyles 'weren't good enough for him' (a statement later echoed by Captain Boyle—'We're not good enough for him'). Juno thinks that Joxer and Maisie Madigan must have alienated him. She makes it clear that Mary had known Bentham in secret before the will, which explains why she had been so unloving to Jerry in the first act—'you knew Bentham, an' I'd ha' known nothin' about it if it hadn't bin for the will'. Mary expresses her love for Bentham—'he wasn't the man poor Jerry was, but I couldn't help loving him, all the same. . . . The best man for a woman is the one for whom he has the most love, and Charlie had it all'. Mary and Juno are not completely close yet—Juno asks why Mary likes to hide everything from her; Mary's reply hurts her: 'It would have been useless to tell you—you wouldn't understand'.

Many things in this act have gone back to their state in Act I. Juno and Captain Boyle are bickering, once more about money; she says they are 'up to our ears in debt' as she nags at him to get up. He has pains in his legs and is drinking again—she accuses him of being carried in drunk the night before. The money has not yet materialised—'It's nearly two months since we heard of the will, an' the money seems as far off as ever'. They owe twenty pounds to the grocer, and Juno is once more afraid to face him. Their possessions begin to disappear. Needle Nugent is the first to take what he has supplied on credit; he comes with Joxer to take away the suit he has made for Captain Boyle. He is also the bearer of bad news who tells us that the will has been wrongly drawn up, to cover all first and second cousins and not just Captain Boyle and one other; the money will never come. He reveals too that Captain Boyle already knows this; his failure to tell anyone has been the ultimate sham. By choosing this conversation between Nugent and Joxer to make these points clear, O'Casey avoids the 'announcement' of the failure of the money to the major characters and the audience simultaneously. Now we wait for the news to come out into the open.

Joxer betrays his friend behind his back with Needle Nugent: he lets him in, connives at taking away the suit and declares 'it's very seldom he escapes me'. Joxer feels he has the right to steal the Captain's stout as Nugent has to take back his suit: the Captain's offences have been forgetting his friends and forgetting God (hardly of importance to Joxer), and acting too grand—'the way Juno an' him's been throwin' their weight about for the last few months!'

Everyone who comes on stage is menacing: Needle Nugent as he claims his suit, Joxer as he cross-questions Captain Boyle about the will; Maisie Madigan who takes the gramophone, throughout the play the symbol of false luxury, as the votive light is the symbol of false security. Now Captain Boyle is being stripped of his borrowed peacock's plumage; the resentment his false grandeur has caused is expressed by Maisie Madigan who wants to shake the money out of him: 'You're not goin' to be swankin' it like a paycock with Maisie Madigan's money—I'll pull some o' the gorgeous feathers out o' your tail'. The rumour is out; Boyle is stripped for all to see as an 'infernal rogue an' damned liar' in Joxer's bitter words—'Sure you can't believe a word that comes out o' your mouth'. Johnny too enters to scold his father; he sees the end of this exchange and accuses him of 'making a show of us all' with Joxer.

The stripping of the Boyles' self-respect continues: Juno comes back from the doctor's with the news that Mary is pregnant. Their selfish reactions give a definite insight into their characters. After his initial muddle—'my God, what'll Bentham say when he hears that?'—Captain Boyle's reflex is that he will suffer the shame of her action: 'Amn't I afther goin' through enough without havin' to go through this!' As he has been tempted out of his class by money, so has Mary by books; 'What did th' likes of her, born in a tenement house, want with readin? Her readin's afther bringin' her to a nice pass'. His image for everything going wrong suggests the breaking up of their home: 'Her an' her readin'! That's more o' the' blasted nonsense that has the house fallin' down on top of us!' Johnny's reaction is inhuman and somewhat surprising in one who so far has seemed limp and timorous. His callous 'She should be dhriven out o' th' house she's brought disgrace on' reminds us of his treachery: he is betraying a member of his family as he betrayed a member of his battalion. Only Juno sees that it is Mary who will suffer, not they. She is protective and stands up to Captain Boyle's bluster. He has forfeited his rights to 'tell her off': 'You'll say nothin' to her, Jack; ever since she left school she's earned her livin', an' your fatherly care never troubled the poor girl'. If he does speak, Mary will leave, and Juno will go with her. She deflates her son's outburst with 'Hush, you, Johnny'.

Juno is more shaken by the next blow, delivered by Boyle. She and Johnny do not yet know about the failure of the will, the removal of money as a means of escape. To her, Mary's pregnancy has been manageable up to now because 'all we have to do is to leave this place quietly an' go somewhere where we're not known an' nobody'll be the wiser'. Her 'But Jack, when we get the money' reveals the vistas of freedom promised by the will. We remember that Johnny's immediate reaction to the news of the legacy in Act I was 'We'll be able to get out o' this place now, an' go somewhere we're not known'; it is for this reason that he is so fierce about the 'loss' of it and so hostile to his father for mismanaging it and running them into debt 'to fill yourself with beer'. His bitter 'Oh, if it's thrue, I'm done with you, for you're worse than me sisther Mary' heralds the disintegration of the family as they turn on each other and drive each other out. Captain Boyle's derisive remark 'Oh, a nice son, an' a nicer daughter I have' as he turns to his old standby Joxer is echoed by Johnny's 'I've a nice sisther, an' a nice father'. Each sees himself as central: 'not one o' yous, not one o' yous, have any thought for me'. Johnny even turns on his mother—'You're to blame yourself ... givin' him his own way in everything ... why didn't you look afther th' money'. Juno, now understanding why Bentham has left Mary, and that there is 'not even a middlin' honest man left in th' world', acknowledges her own central rôle and the strain of it. 'If you don't whisht, Johnny, you'll drive me mad. Who has kep' th' home together for the past few years—only me? An' who'll have to bear th' biggest part o' this throuble but me?' The expected rôles in the family are hard to dislodge. As the furniture men take the furniture away, Johnny asks his mother to bring his father back to stop them; despite his father's failure he feels he ought to be there to protect them. As Juno goes to get him, she meets Mary and tells her that the will has failed them; she is the last to hear officially, but has already heard the rumour. In fact Mary does not react at all to the news. Nor does she reply to Johnny's recriminations. Nor, when Jerry returns after all the time that has elapsed since the first act, does she answer him at first. But when he announces that Juno has told him 'everything', and that his love for her is 'greater and deeper than ever', she tells him 'all that is over now'. For a moment it seems that Jerry is the only character in the play with his 'principles' still intact. He pleads as a lover 'What does it matter what has happened? We are young enough to be able to forget all those things', and as a Socialist: 'With Labour, Mary, humanity is above everything; we are the Leaders in the fight for a new life'. Her momentary hope that he alone of the men will not reject her is touching and ironic in the face of his cruel

'My God, Mary, have you fallen as low as that?' His humanitarian principles have been as empty as all the rest; his love has been as imaginary as her father's and brother's affection. Mary herself shows humility, dignity and simplicity in her reply to his awkward apology: 'Let us say no more, Jerry; I don't blame you for thinkin' it's terrible'. But she sees clearly his betrayal of their principles: 'it's only as I expected. Your humanity is just as narrow as the humanity of the others'. She detains him to talk about the verses he once read at a Socialist lecture about 'Humanity's strife with Nature'; he fails her even in this by not remembering them. They are verses of chaos and conflict about ugliness superimposed on beauty, with harsh discordant images and awkward phrases. She quotes his own words to him at length but he leaves without a word; communication between them is utterly broken.

It is an indication of Johnny's self-absorption that this parting means nothing to him except that Jerry could have stopped the furniture men taking away their possessions if Mary had not told him the truth; he accuses her savagely of 'burnin' to tell every one' of the shame she has brought on them. His bitterness drives her out—it is unbearable.

As the furniture men get on with their job of stripping the rooms bare, the play explodes into action, symbolic and actual. The votive light goes out and Johnny shouts in fear; then he gives an agonising cry, 'Mother o' God, there's a shot I'm afther gettin''. He thinks has has felt a pain in his breast 'like the tearin' by of a bullet': this time his tormentors are heralded by violence. The two Irregulars are the concrete reality of something we been expecting throughout the play, as terse, merciless and unyielding as Johnny has feared. They have a word to say to him; they have no time to waste. Every protest that Johnny makes is thrown back with a contemptuous contradiction: 'Yous wouldn't shoot an oul' comrade': 'Poor Tancred was an oul' comrade'; Johnny's lost arm is countered by Tancred's lost life. Their ominous question 'Have you your beads?' is the confirmation of their sentence of death. His rosary will help him to pray as he dies, and will be a token of faith in his dead fingers. He uses what mechanical aids his church affords, calling on the Sacred Heart of Jesus, ever-present in this play until the extinguishing of the votive light. He says the Hail Mary, the prayer we last heard at Tancred's funeral, choosing the lines 'be with me now in the agonies o' death'.

Into the final moments of this act O'Casey piles the resolution of Mary's story and Juno's, the confirmation of Johnny's death and the reaffirmation of the eternal worthlessness of Captain Boyle and Joxer. Juno and Mary wait in the almost empty room for news of Johnny and

Juno again imagines her own madness: 'If anything ud happen to poor Johnny, I think I'd lose me mind'. Maisie Madigan brings the news that the police want to see her because a body has been found. Mary's instinct towards Juno is maternal for the first time: 'Oh mother, mother, me poor, darlin' mother', a protectiveness reciprocated: 'you'll shortly have your own throuble to bear'. Johnny has been identified, ironically, by his missing arm, that talisman of his heroism: the wound he got honourably defending an ideal now confirms his traitor's death. Juno does not go mad; she keeps control while Mary turns on God: 'There isn't a God! There isn't a God; if there was He wouldn't let these things happen'. Juno's practical side sees the will of God as impotent against man—the Humanity that ruined Nature in Jerry's verses. She decides to go away with Mary, and breaks her links with Captain Boyle unhistrionically; he can shift for himself now—he'll be hopeless till the end of his days. She has done what she can in this home; now life will be a room lent by her sister, and herself and Mary working together for the sake of the baby. To Mary's sentimental and conventional 'My poor little child that'll have no father' she advances the practical, optimistic and feminist 'It'll have what's far betther—it'll have two mothers'. In the last link with her 'old' family, she plans to see Johnny's dead body, from which Mary recoils. From reproaching herself for upsetting the pregnant girl by suggesting it, Juno goes on to reproach herself for not having had true sympathy for Mrs Tancred in the same situation. 'Why didn't I remember that then he wasn't a Diehard or a Stater, but only a poor dead son!' (she did in fact at the time say 'no matther whose friend or enemy he was, he was her poor son'). She consciously identifies herself with Mrs Tancred as a mother who, remembering the pain of childbirth, now brings her son untimely to the grave in greater pain. She echoes her prayer 'Sacred Heart o' Jesus, take away our hearts o' stone, and give us hearts o' flesh! Take away this murdherin' hate an' give us Thine own eternal love!' She too turns to the Blessed Virgin—but where was she when Johnny was riddled with bullets? She has failed, as all pleas to God have failed in the play.

When Juno and Mary have left for their new and optimistic life, Captain Boyle and Joxer come back drunk to the old life, their money gone, their songs in snatches, their boasts proliferating as they did in Act I. Captain Boyle vaguely notices that the blinds are down and the chairs gone, but does not perceive that his family has gone too. He relates the disorder in himself and his home to his country—'the chairs'll have to steady themselves ... the counthry'll have to steady itself; Irelan' sober is Irelan' free'. His patriotic boast of having taken part in the Easter Rising of 1916 like his son has as little conviction as his seafaring myths. As his son lies dead somewhere he spins a yarn about his Commandant dying in his arms, which Joxer answers by referring to a romantic and irrelevant Irish novel. He decides yet again, in the bitterest unconscious irony, that 'th'whole worl's in a terrible state o' chassis'; he does not realise how chaotic it truly is, how empty his life has been left. We see how much truer is the catchphrase than they realise.

In this act the central bond between Mary and Juno is established and remains firm. Around these two women all others fall away; Bentham, Captain Boyle, Johnny and Jerry all reject Mary; the links between Juno and her son are broken by his death, between Juno and her husband broken by his failure to stand by his family.

So the four intermingled plots of the play have been resolved: Mary has been abandoned by Bentham and by Jerry; Johnny has been branded guilty and executed; the will has evaporated; and Juno has stepped away from her Paycock towards the new generation.

NOTES AND GLOSSARY

**so great together:** so close
**bin:** been
**let out:** admitted
**a frog's march:** to be carried face down by four men holding an arm or leg each (OED)
**Sloan's Liniment:** proprietary cream for rubbing muscles
**the *Messenger*:** *The Messenger of the Sacred Heart*: a Catholic monthly magazine with religious stories, prayers, lists of favours granted etc
**News o' the World:** a salacious English weekly newspaper
**me pipe I'll smoke ...:** misquotation from a popular ballad, 'The Star of the County Down'. It should be 'no pipe I'll smoke and no horse I'll yoke/'Till my plough is a rust-coloured brown,/And a smiling bride by my own fireside/Sits the Star of the County Down'
**a red rex:** a penny (copper coin with the king's head)
**a make:** a halfpenny
**an honest man's the noblest work o' God:** popular quotation from *Essay on Man* by Alexander Pope (1688–1744)
**man's inhumanity to man:** quotation from 'Man was made to mourn: A dirge' by Robert Burns (1759–96).
**a barny:** a chat
**formularies** she means formalities
**she has ... a sup taken:** she's drunk

**Come in the evenin'** . . .: quoted from *The Welcome*, a song written by Thomas Davis (1814–45) for the Nationalist newspaper *The Nation* in 1841: 'Come in the evening or come in the morning,/Come when you're looked for, or come without warning/Kisses and welcome you'll find here before you,/And the oft'ner you come here, the more I'll adore you'. Maisie Madigan is not, of course, a welcome guest on her present mission

**The anchor's weighed** . . .: romantic song from the opera *The Americans* (1811) by John Braham (1777–1856): it continues ' "Weep not, my love", I trembling said, "Doubt not a constant heart like mine . . ." ', in ironic contrast with Joxer's inconstancy

**a gradle:**    a great deal

**The Little Flower:**    Saint Theresa of Lisieux (1873–1897) revered for her simplicity, humility and endurance of suffering, and known as 'the Little Flower of Jesus'

**a Child of Mary:**    a member of a children's religious confraternity dedicated to the Virgin Mary which had blue ribbons, uniforms and banners

**swank:**    dandy

**whack:**    share

**banjax:**    mess

**whisht:**    be quiet

**Irregular:**    the Diehard or extreme section of the Irish Republican Army

**Sean**    Irish equivalent of John

**your beads:**    Rosary beads, an aid to prayer in the Roman Catholic church; one's beads were also twined around one's fingers in one's coffin

**Stater:**    Free Stater

**The Last o' the Mohicans:** *The Last of the Mohicans*, an adventure story of North American Indians by the American novelist James Fenimore Cooper (1789–1857)

**Put all your troubles:** misquotation of a marching and recruiting song sung in the First World War and also by the British occupying troops in Ireland, which makes its use here incongruous. 'What's the use of worrying?/It never was worth while, so,/Pack up your troubles in your old kit bag,/And smile, smile smile'.

**flying column:**    special commando force

**Breathes there a man:** misquotation of a patriotic stanza from 'The Lay of the Last Minstrel' by Sir Walter Scott (1771–1832): 'Breathes there the man, with soul so dead,/ Who never to himself hath said,/This is my own, my native land!'

**Willie Reilly an' his own Colleen Bawn:** *Willy Reilly and his dear Coleen Bawn* (1855) a romantic novel by the Irish writer William Carleton (1796–1869) about Ireland in Penal times, when Irish Catholics were being persecuted; in it a Protestant heiress elopes with a poor Roman Catholic.

# Part 3

# Commentary

## Themes

### Structure and subjects

*Juno and the Paycock* has a simple three-act structure, with no division into scenes. The only variation is a fall and rise of the curtain at the end of the last act, allowing the final action of the play to take place an hour later. The four linked plots follow this structure, each act marking a well-defined stage in each story. Johnny is nervous in Act I, incriminated in Act II, executed in Act III. Mary is linked with Jerry in Act I, with Bentham in Act II, pregnant and abandoned by both in Act III. The will is announced in Act I, falsely realised in Act II, and withdrawn in Act III. Juno and Captain Boyle are antagonists in Act I, almost friends in Act II and separated in Act III. These four simple plots are closely interwoven, their comic and tragic elements succeeding each other to give continual changes of mood and pace. A tragi-comedy is not merely a play containing funny and serious parts, but one in which the comic and the tragic are integrated so that each affects the other, the comedy throwing the tragedy into relief, the tragic basis giving the comedy an ironic depth. *Juno and the Paycock* is a tragi-comedy; we see in it scenes and situations that are superficially funny but of the deepest tragic implication.

O'Casey is sparing in his use of characters and speech. People are described in succinct comment by others, past events summed up in a few words, often by Juno. Changes in relationships take place between the acts—Mary finishes with Jerry and takes up with Bentham between Acts I and II; she is deserted by Bentham between Acts II and III. The characters advance and retreat—Jerry is not in Act II, Bentham is only briefly in Act I, and not in Act III. Mary is not present when her pregnancy is announced. Effects are achieved economically, with short appearances, and brief reactions to even the major events in the play. Johnny's terse comment on Mary's pregnancy, 'she should be driven from the house', reveals his character beyond a doubt. The repetition of certain situations provides a double commentary; Mrs Tancred and her son's funeral are echoed by Juno and her son's death; the meeting between Mary and Johnny in Act I has its ironic repetition in Act III when, despite his protests of eternal love, he rejects her.

The play is realistic in its detail: stockings, cupboards, trousers and shovels give it a firm base in reality. It has not the surrealism of O'Casey's controversial later plays such as *The Silver Tassie* or *Cock-a-Doodle-Dandy* or of the play he had already written, the one-act *Kathleen Listens In*. But to O'Casey absolute realism was impossible and undesirable in the theatre; the dramatist's task was to heighten reality. Side by side with the strict realism of the play's settings, characters and dialogue is a strong yet simple poetic symbolism of everyday objects: the protecting votive light that goes out just before Johnny is taken away; the statue with the bleeding heart that Johnny 'sees' as Tancred's wounded body; the gramophone that represents Juno's yearning for luxury and gaiety. Even certain names carry symbolic overtones: Juno, the quarrelling wife of Jove, patroness of marriage and childbirth, Tancred, the nationalist hero. The use of the Virgin Mary has this symbolic quality; and indeed the use of literary and musical references has such significant precision that it could be called symbolic. These are combined with characters and speeches that are natural yet heightened; and a melodramatic series of events that seem natural, given the horrific and inhuman outer setting of civil war.

O'Casey's purpose in the play, as in *The Shadow of a Gunman* and *The Plough and the Stars*, was to show the emptiness of jingoistic nationalism, too besotted with heroics to see that the Irish nation's true oppressors were poverty and ignorance. He is concerned with the greater humanity, including the Irish and here exemplified by them. O'Casey's interest lay in freeing all men from such oppression, through Labour, not through nationalism. He shows Ireland as a battleground over which successive fights are being fought, taking their toll of Irish youth for causes that will not improve its condition. He looks towards the future generations of Ireland rather than her past dead heroes. And within the broad framework of the liberation of a class, he puts forward an Ibsenist claim for the liberation of the individual.

O'Casey's originality in this play, as in his other early work, was to give a voice to a class never heard seriously on the stage before—the Dublin poor. This voice was as individual as that given by John Millington Synge to the Irish peasants of the Aran Islands, and more realistic. In this voice he claimed the right of all men to work, to live in dignity, to be freed from ignorance and poverty. And by this voice he represented his Dublin characters as being as far from the romantic idea of the nationalist hero as they were from the traditional funny, harmless stage Irishman. He shows the reality of the Easter Rising cult heroes—Johnny maimed in body and cowardly of mind; former Irish comrades now fighting each other as bloodily as they had the English only a few years previously.

As for the stage Irishman, O'Casey does not avoid him, as many Irish writers claim to do. He uses him as skilfully as his first comic master, Dion Boucicault (1822-1890); he allows Captain Boyle and Joxer all his characteristics but he shows them as corrupting and degraded, not harmless. The stage Irishman is feckless, devious, ignorant, disloyal, laughable. Captain Boyle's unwillingness to work, his 'pains in his legs', are comic for the moment, but they are symptoms of that extreme irresponsibility which is one of the tragic themes of the play. Everyone strives to see him as the head of the family, but he is incapable of supporting them materially or morally. Joxer is dishonest, sycophantic and revengeful. Their self-indulgent escapes into words, fantasy and drink are evasions of reality and responsibility. We are caught in the act of laughing at them and made to see the ugliness behind the joke.

O'Casey's practical achievement was to make people who saw the play question their fixed principles in a country that had been divided between unionists and nationalists for over a century. He was not speaking only to the nationalists but to the many Irish people who felt it their duty to be loyal to England (150,000 fought voluntarily for England in the 1914-18 War). O'Casey demonstrates the futility and horror of Irishmen killing each other over a treaty; the misguidedness of those who like Johnny are committed to the fight, those like Captain Boyle who disclaim all responsibility, and those who like Bentham are callous and impersonal: 'The only way to deal with a mad dog is to to kill it'.

## The historical background

The historical and sociological background of the play is very skilfully woven in with its action. The political situation in 1922 was that after more than a century of British rule, and many years of fighting and negotiating for an independent Irish republic, a treaty between Britain and Ireland had been signed, giving Ireland limited independence as a Free State. Entrenched or 'Diehard' Republicans refused to accept this treaty and were engaged in a civil war with those who did. As in *The Shadow of a Gunman* and *The Plough and the Stars*, we are continually aware of events going on outside. The funeral of Tancred comes closest; but Johnny's battalion is manoeuvring nearby, bodies are being found in the hills, newspapers are full of casualties, and five men in this one tenement have been killed or wounded.

The political situation is evident not only in large matters like Johnny's story, but in small points like Joxer being afraid to look out of the window for fear of 'a bullet in the kisser'. And 'the troubles', as they were called, have seeped into the vocabulary and imagery of the characters' speech. Captain Boyle's announcement 'Today, Joxer, there's goin' to be issued a proclamation be me, establishin' an independent Republic, an' Juno'll have to take an oath of allegiance', his 'more throubles in our native land' and Joxer's bitter comment about him 'goin' about like a mastherpiece of the Free State Country' all reflect current events.

The past background is also introduced by slight allusions that mount up to a formidable whole. Maisie Madigan's account of herself singing 'An' You'll Remember Me' is dramatically overshadowed by the barber who gave the party, who adjusted his pole to the Irish colours for the Republicans and the English ones for the British 'Black and Tans': 'the barber ... that, afther Easther Week, hung out a green, white an' orange pole, an' then, when the Tans started their Jazz dancin' whipped it in agen, an' stuck out a red, white, an' blue wan instead, givin' as an excuse that a barber's pole was strictly non-political'. This shows the intrusion of the wars into everyday life (as Juno describes the 'CID men burstin' into your room') and the opportunism they breed (like that of Needle Nugent who goes to Republican funerals by day and sews Free State police uniforms by night). It is this level of politics that O'Casey explores—not the promise of 'Ireland free' but the reality of the Irish captive to a handful of hotheads on either side, and opportunists between.

## Jingoism

One of O'Casey's targets in *Juno and the Paycock* is jingoism, or blustering patriotism (originally support for a belligerent British foreign policy in 1878, encapsulated in a popular song with the refrain 'By Jingo'). It is expressed in the spurious nationalism of Needle Nugent: 'Have none o' yous any respect for the Irish people's National regard for the dead', which has no regard for the living, as Juno points out. The jingoistic counter to Johnny's 'haven't I done enough for Ireland?' is 'no man can do enough for Ireland'. Johnny in himself incarnates the fatal effects of jingoistic principles taken to their conclusion. It is against jingoistic all-or-nothing principles to accept the Free State Treaty because it excludes Ulster and does not give Ireland total autonomy. Johnny takes the motto of a Sinn Fein journal, 'Ireland unfree will never be at peace', and expresses it more aggressively: 'Ireland only half free'll never be at peace while she has a son left to pull a trigger', One of O'Casey's points is that the logical consequence of jingoism is that Ireland will soon not have any sons to pull triggers; they will all be dead or maimed. Johnny is full of jargon—'a principle's a principle'; but he fails in the elementary principle of loyalty and betrays a comrade.

Captain Boyle epitomises the most hypocritical aspects of jingoism. His sentimental view of the 'memory of the dead' has the priests working against the patriots: 'We don't forget, we don't forget them things, Joxer. If they've taken everything else from us, Joxer, they've left us our memory'. Ironically, he has forgotten by the next act, and changes his tune completely: 'as far as I know the History o' me country, the priests was always in the van of the fight for Irelan's freedom'. Like Nugent the opportunist, he wants to profit from the patriotism of others—'It's a curious way to reward Johnny be makin' his poor oul' father work'. Jingoism is as much an escape from reality as his other fantasies: his last drunken speech is jingoistic: 'I done me bit in Easther week. Commandant Kelly died in them arms. Tell me Volunteer Butties . . . that I died for Ireland'. In his blind romantic jingoism, he cannot see that his home is deserted, his family dead or gone. Everyone glibly talks of 'dying for Ireland'. The neighbour who says of Tancred 'He died a noble death an' we'll bury him like a king' considers that a recompense for his mother's loss. To his 'It's a sad journey we're goin' on, but God's good, an' the Republicans won't be always down', Mrs Tancred answers with personal disregard for the clichés of republicanism: 'What good is that to me now? Whether they're up or down—it won't bring me darlin' boy from the grave'.

## The poverty line

There is a poverty line below which it is difficult to live and above which the poor cannot rise because they have no capital; they can only borrow at interest, buy uneconomically in small quantities, and sink further. O'Casey shows his characters living below both a material and an intellectual poverty line. The Boyles live on credit, no doubt at exorbitant interest. They owe 'oul' Murphy' twenty pounds—'What'll we do if he refuses to give us any more on tick?' One of the functions of the will in the play is to show the sudden effects of the supposed release from poverty, which robs men of gaiety as well as of dignity. The Boyles run to tinsel, parties and gramophones in search of joy. They also see the money as a means of escaping from the tenement, the environment that drags them down. The stage directions describe the adverse effects of poverty on Juno's looks and outlook, and on Mary's speech and mind, despite her reading. This is done because O'Casey wants to show that there is also an intellectual poverty line, above which it is equally difficult to rise, with little education, and in the face of the ignorance which mocks and threatens. Captain Boyle embodies the power that 'holds Mary back' as her reading urges her forwards. He blames all her troubles on her books—'what did th' likes of her, born in a tenement house, want with readin'?'

If O'Casey succeeded in giving a voice to the slum dwellers of Dublin as a class, he also demonstrates how hard a struggle it is for members of that group to have an identity. They have no privacy in which to develop; everything from putting on one's trousers to mourning one's son has to be done in public. A Joxer or a Maisie Madigan is always at the ready, wanted or unwanted. People lose their individuality; they are introduced as the 'front parlour neighbour', the 'top floor back', 'Mrs Tancred of the two-pair back'—these multitudinous families are in a house originally intended for one. Johnny expresses the immediate irritation of having someone 'thrampin' about like a horse' over one's head; even Jerry's love scene with Mary is played out within earshot of Captain Boyle. Being drawn in willy-nilly to one's neighbour's doings forces one into the self-protective callousness expressed not only by Captain Boyle ('them things . . . don't affect us') but also by the usually maternal Juno who sees the threat of the Tancreds' CID raids drawing her family into trouble. Her poverty impedes her humanity. (Her hard words about Mrs Tancred for which she later reproaches herself, 'she brought it on herself', are prompted by fear and the need to protect her own family.) Poverty also corrupts Joxer and Captain Boyle; unemployment breeds the indolence, drunkenness and incapacity for work that they display.

## The Labour movement

The Labour movement is fundamental to *Juno and the Paycock*. O'Casey's work for the 1913 lockout and his admiration for Jim Larkin gave him very high ideals for it; here he shows the forces against which it had to contend in Ireland. Captain Boyle is anti-Labour, idle and drunk, hardworking only in the avoidance of work, living on the State. He is a parasite on whom lives another parasite, Joxer. Juno is a hard worker but fears trade unionism. Johnny is so crippled that he cannot work. Mary loses her original interest in the principles of trade unionism when she is with Bentham—although it is she who keeps its ideals. Jerry, the representative of the Labour movement in the play, fails in his private life to live up to O'Casey's (and his own) humanitarian principles.

The Labour movement affects these different characters in differing degrees. Jerry's job, his principles and even his love for Mary are all based on his trade unionism. In his last scene with her he says 'With Labour, Mary, humanity is above everything; we are the Leaders in the fight for a new life'; this is O'Casey's own ideal of the world Labour movement. But he has already indicated in the stage directions that Jerry has not the depth of intellect or compassion necessary for the ideal: 'He is a type, becoming very common now in the Labour movement, of a mind knowing enough to make the mass of his associates, who know less, a power, and too little to broaden that power for the benefit of all'. In the course of the play we would not have known this until the moment when he rejects Mary and shows his lack of true humanity—which should be extended to the individual as well as to the class.

The Labour movement also has a great influence on Mary. She has worked since she left school. She ranges herself against the bosses, and is active enough to come out on strike. She is affected by its jargon—'stand up for your principles'; she has embraced its ideals and even its literature—she can quote entire the verses from Jerry's speech. Her attempt to educate herself is in line with Labour thinking.

Mary sees the need for humanity ('we couldn't let her walk the streets') and she sees that it is not just love for herself but humanity that Jerry lacks—'your humanity is just as narrow as the humanity of the others'.

Juno represents traditional short-term reaction against trade unionism—a strike will cause many to be out of work instead of just one; 'when the employers sacrifice wan victim, the trade unions go wan betther be sacrificin' a hundred'. This old-fashioned shortsightedness corresponds with her improvident buying on credit. She works, and believes in work—but she is interested in her own family to the exclusion of all others, which is against the true socialist ethic. She sees that Johnny has been deprived of the right to work by his nationalism: 'you lost your best principle, me boy, when you lost your arm; them's the only sort o' principles that's any good to a workin' man'. Joxer is a professional sponger, Captain Boyle a chronic escaper of work. They illustrate a two-way process; mostly there is not enough work, so there are many unemployed. But after the inertia of years out of work, living on the unemployment dole and the health insurance, the unemployed man will not take work even if it appears. Man's right, need and duty to work are major issues in the play.

## The Church

Although he was a Protestant, O'Casey had lived among Dublin Roman Catholics all his life. In a culture where the division between Catholic and Protestant was very marked, both socially and in matters of faith and methods of worship, he was unusually tolerant. His familiarity with the ritual and observances of the Catholic church is apparent in many religious allusions. Catholicism is so much a part of Irish life that it is logical for it to penetrate the play at all levels. The priests are referred to in their social and political functions as much as in their religious mission. Religion in the shape of God, Christ and the Virgin Mary, is seen as an inspiration and a comfort. It supplies a wealth of everyday vocabulary, imagery and oaths. Above all, it is a potent source of symbolism, counterpointing the action. The five functions of religion in the play are thus: social, political, spiritual, linguistic and symbolic.

**Social** Father Farrell is sneeringly represented by Joxer as Captain Boyle's ever-grinning 'guardian angel', ready to shake hands with him only when he is rich. But in reality he tries to get him 'a start' by finding him a job when he is poor, though without thanks—'that's what the clergy want, Joxer—work, work, work for me an' you; havin' us mulin' from mornin' to night, so that they may be in betther fettle when they come hoppin' round for their dues'. But there are some more esoteric social functions of the Church—the confraternities, sodalities and children's groups so frequently referred to. The 'prayer-spoutin, craw-thumpin' Confraternity men' were such a group, dedicated to the Sacred Heart, and Mary's having been 'a Child o' Mary' refers to a children's confraternity, with blue uniform sashes and banners. The links between these church groups and nationalist army groups were often very close. O'Casey himself was drawn into the nationalist movement by joining a young people's social club based on a Catholic school. He draws a parallel between nationalist and church armies with their ribbons and banners and oaths.

**Political** The rôle of the Catholic Church in Irish politics is seen by Captain Boyle according to his finances. Poor, he accuses the priests of preventing the starving people from stealing corn during the famine, of letting down the Fenian rebels, and of destroying Parnell. When he feels their equal because he is 'rich', they have led the fight for Ireland's freedom. He acknowledges their influence: 'the clergy always had too much power over the people in this unfortunate country'. It is in this context that Juno feels that the Church should be working with the people to make the new Irish Free State: 'when we got the makin' of our own laws I thought we'd never stop to look behind us, but instead of that we never stopped to look before us! If the people ud folley up their religion betther there'd be a betther chance for us!'

**Spiritual** We are constantly reminded of religion as a source of spiritual comfort in the play—'Merciful Jesus, have pity on me'. 'Great God, have mercy on me! Blessed Mother o' God, shelter me, shelther your son! ... merciful Jesus, have pity on me!' cries Johnny when he has 'seen' Tancred kneeling in front of the statue. It is particularly the Virgin Mary who is seen as a protectress. For Johnny her picture is all-important: 'The wan inside to St Anthony isn't enough, but he must have another wan to the Virgin here!' But every prayer made for help, succour or protection seems ironically to fail. The two bereaved mothers, Mrs Tancred and Juno, each say 'Blessed Virgin, where were you when me darlin' son was riddled with bullets'; and for all his praying, Johnny is not protected, and is led off still praying 'Mother o' God, pray for me—be with me now in the agonies o' death! ... Hail, Mary, full o' grace ... the Lord is ... with Thee,' an echo of the Hail Mary last heard at Tancred's funeral.

It is Mary who voices the fact that their prayers to the Church fail them, when they hear that Johnny is dead: 'Oh, it's thrue, it's thrue what Jerry Devine says—there isn't a God, there isn't a God; if there was He wouldn't let these things happen!' Juno's first response is pragmatic: 'Mary, you mustn't say them things! We'll want all the help we can get from God an' His Blessed Mother now'. This corresponds to a standard self-protective concern with rituals, statues and votive lights—Boyle mentions 'all your prayin' to St Anthony an' The Little Flower' (Saint Theresa). But she continues with a socialist or human-itarian argument: 'These things have nothin' to do with the Will o' God. Ah, what can God do agen the stupidity o' men!' This is the argument of O'Casey the humanist—like Jerry the Labourite, 'all man an' no God'. Only in this belief can anything be done to save humanity; it is 'man's inhumanity to man' that causes suffering, evil and poverty, and that is in strife with nature. As Juno says, 'with all our churches an' religions, the worl's not a bit the betther'. It is man himself who must save his fellows, not images, prayers, rituals or God.

To illustrate the inherent weakness of religion, O'Casey juxtaposes theosophy and Roman Catholicism as parallel religions. Captain Boyle says of Bentham's theosophical creed 'isn't all religions curious?'. In a Dublin where Yeats and his friends were dabbling in spiritualism, the idea of Life Breath, Prana and Yogi was laughable but not unheard of.

Bentham explains theosophy as a quest for happiness; technically it is a 'wisdom-religion', a philosophical system claiming to have divine wisdom and the knowledge of the existence and nature of the deity. Bentham's definition is ironic: 'the happiness of man depends on sympathy in spirit'—a quality singularly lacking in Dublin in 1922, particularly in the man who wishes to kill Republicans like mad dogs. Mental exercises (comparable with the ritual and prayers of the Catholic religion) could give you powers denied to others 'like seeing things that happen miles and miles away'—again ironic in Ireland where men's need is to see properly the dreadful things that are happening under their noses.

**Linguistic** Religion is used in speech in the play in several ways. First, it is a reflex verbal response of shock or surprise: 'what in the name o' God', 'Holy God' when a bottle of stout is stolen. It has become cheapened into oaths: 'I can swear on all the holy prayer books', 'For God's sake, let us have no more o' this talk'. (Such exclamations are not always meaningless: when Juno says 'God help us' or Maisie 'God send it's not Johnny', they mean it.) It is also a source of imagery: 'things . . . that no mortal man should speak of that knows his catechism' or 'that man'll be lookin' for somethin' on th' day o' Judgement'. And there are frequent echoes of the Catholic prayerbook, as in Mrs Tancred's 'give us thine own eternal love'.

**Symbolic** Religion provides several recurrent symbols: the Virgin Mary, the votive light, the Sacred Heart, the prayers and hymns. Johnny's deepest feelings are related to the Virgin and to the votive light, which burns all through the play until it is extinguished before Johnny's arrest. He constantly seeks its protection—'is the light lightin' before the picture o' the Virgin?' but far from protecting him, it illuminates his guilty vision: 'I seen him . . . I seen Robbie Tancred kneelin' down before the statue an' the red light shinin' on him . . . an' I seen the woun's bleeding' in his breast'. The representation of the Sacred Heart in popular art is of a bleeding heart exposed on the breast; here Tancred's wounds are related to the sacrificial wounds of Christ. It is Bentham the non-Christian who dares to look at the statue and reports 'Everything's just as it was—the light burning bravely before the statue'; but to us, things are not the same. Johnny's guilt has been revealed by the Virgin and her light. The extinguishing of the light also symbolises the emptying of the Boyles' home: when a Catholic chapel is abandoned, it is deconsecrated, its altar furniture removed, and its sanctuary lamp extinguished. The Virgin Mary also represents bereaved motherhood;

her son was killed like Juno's and Mrs Tancred's. The reiteration of prayers and hymns counterpoints the action with an easily grasped symbolism, like the 'Hail Mary' sung at Tancred's funeral as the Mobilizer comes for Johnny, who later repeats it himself as he is taken to be punished for Tancred's death. Even the rosary beads he must take with him are at the same time an emblem of prayer and an emblem of death; it is customary to entwine a dead person's beads in his fingers in the coffin.

# The characters

## Juno

Juno's outstanding characteristic, which no other person in the play possesses, is her awareness. She is not lost in principles like her son and daughter nor in fantasies like Captain Boyle and Joxer, but is conscious of what is going on in real life around her. From this springs her practicality, her rôle as explicator of events and introducer of people to each other. It also lets her see that political events affect them all: 'Sure, if it's not our business, I don't know whose business it is'.

More unusually, her awareness extends to herself, from her place in the family ('I don't know what any o' yous ud do without your ma') to her own lapses in sensitivity in suggesting that Mary go to see Johnny's body with her, or in failing to understand Mrs Tancred's grief. She is aware, too, of the pressures on her own mind. More than once she sees madness threatening her: ('I will go mad if Johnny dies', 'If anything ud happen to poor Johnny, I think I'd lose me mind'). She does not in fact go mad. Her practical side asserts itself to noble effect; she and Mary will work for the next generation, Mary's child. Juno, with her clear vision, sees that to do this she must leave her husband and her now-empty home; the future depends on her freeing herself from them.

The momentum of the play is all towards this movement of strength and humanity in Juno. She is always a matriarchal figure, but at the beginning of the play she has not the stature she has developed at the end; a grandeur born of pain, disillusion and grief. The dominating factor of her life at the beginning of the play is poverty. Because of it she must work and see her daughter work while her husband idles; she must grumble and nag and worry. The difference between her possibilities and what her life has limited her to is made clear: 'were circumstances favourable, she would probably be a handsome, active and clever woman'. O'Casey saw his own mother deprived of any luxuries or small pleasures; he wrote bitterly of her death as her first rest in 'Mrs Casside takes a holiday' (in *Inishfallen, Fare Thee Well*). Juno's first 'holiday' in the false riches of the will leads her into materialism and vulgarity; she chooses cheap trappings and a gramophone. Poverty causes much of her bitterness towards her husband; the tension between them is eased when they think they have money. At other times she uses her sharp tongue and vivid images to deflate him: 'your poor wife slavin' to keep the bit in your mouth, an' you gallivantin' about all day like a paycock!' Her 'everybody callin' you Captain, an' you only wanst on the wather' strips him of one of his public masks. But her reaction to the will is 'you won't have to trouble about a job'. This is not ironic; it is linked to her idea of him as the breadwinner, at last bringing money into the house.

Juno has two earthly and two heavenly parallels. Her earthly parallels are Mrs Tancred and Maisie Madigan. The likeness to Maisie Madigan is in her sharpness of tongue, her singing, her generosity and her vulgarity in the moments when she thinks herself rich. Her likeness to Mrs Tancred is as one of a sisterhood of sorrowing mothers; they are overtly compared in Juno's own words, and in her echoing of Mrs Tancred's elegy: 'Maybe I didn't feel sorry enough for Mrs Tancred when her poor son was found as Johnny's been found now ... It's well I remember all that she said—an' it's my turn to say it now'. Her heavenly parallels are with her namesake Juno and with the Virgin Mary. Juno, in Roman mythology the wife of Jupiter, king of the Gods, regarded as the only really married goddess among the Olympians, was the protectress of married women and of childbearers. She, like Mrs Boyle, had frequent quarrels with her husband, and once put him in chains for threatening her; Boyle's infidelity is not with other women but with Joxer, representing loose and irresponsible living. Her heavenly parallel with the Virgin Mary is sustained, particularly in her relations with Johnny. When he calls 'Blessed Mother o' God, shelter me, shelther your son!' it is Juno who 'catches him in her arms'. The more she becomes the noble mother figure of the end of the play, the closer she comes to the mother of Christ whose son was also killed.

Juno also has the ordinary motherly and womanly characteristics. She is protective to her children when they need it, as Johnny always does. She scolds the strong Mary of Act I, but when she is weak, comforts and protects her: 'we'll all have to mind her'. She stands up for her fiercely against Captain Boyle: 'You'll say nothin' to her, Jack; ever since she left school she's earned her livin', an' your fatherly care never throubled the poor girl'. She is the only one in the family who does not consider her own interests in Mary's 'shame'; to Boyle's 'Amn't

I afther goin' through enough' she replies 'What you an' I'll have to go through'll be nothin' to what poor Mary'll have to go through; for you an' me is middlin' old, an' most of our years is spent; but Mary'll have maybe forty years to face an' handle, an' every wan of them'll be tainted with a bitther memory'. This is Juno's generosity of spirit, and her clear-eyed perceptiveness; she alone is not too self-absorbed to see Mary's predicament. At the worst moments, she accepts and takes further her anchor rôle: 'who'll have to bear th' biggest part o' this trouble but me? But whinin' an' whingin' isn't goin' to help'. When she waits for the news of Johnny's death, she asks and answers 'Is me throubles never goin' to be over? . . . I've gone through so much lately, that I feel able for anything'.

Only in one respect is her vision obscured until the end of the play: she seems to have a picture of home and family not as it is but as it should be. Not until the end does she allow herself to see the true disintegration of her family. As she and Mary wait for news of Johnny she says 'maybe it's your father'; but Boyle has failed as husband and as father and just as he was not there to stop the furniture being taken away, he will not be there to support her for their son's death. Her speech continues 'though when I left him in Foley's he was hardly able to lift his head'. This is the moment when she realises 'I've done all I could an' it was all no use—he'll be hopeless till the end of his days'; it is the moment that she realises herself, and the climax of the play. Her resolution that she and Mary will 'work together for the sake of the baby' and her decision to leave Captain Boyle to 'furrage for himself' are not feminist but self-realising. When she counters Mary's 'My poor little child that'll have no father' with a brisk 'It'll have what's far betther—it'll have two mothers', she is not preaching women's liberation, but trying to free Mary from a negative and sentimental attitude, as she is freeing herself from a dead and deadening life by taking a positive, optimistic and humanitarian step into the future.

## Captain Boyle

Captain Boyle is one of the mainsprings of laughter and comedy in the play, yet he is also a major contributor to its tragic side. Superficially, everything about him is funny—his strenuous efforts to avoid working, the pains in his legs, his devious attempts to keep one step ahead of Juno and the accompanying fear that he will not succeed. His language, rhetoric and muddled flow of words are funny; his exaggerations and catchphrases are funny; his exchanges with Joxer are hilarious. Where then does the tragic side come in? First, he is a failure as a father and as a husband; second, he is a representative product of the slums. Poverty breeds lack of work, idleness, drunkenness. It breeds Dublin men with nothing to do but talk. It breeds the self-protective callousness of fear, the ignorance that condemns learning, the false comradeship that has no loyalty, the irresponsibility that makes Captain Boyle fail his family.

He has the same misguided picture of himself as head of the family that Juno clings to. He plays the part with pompous phrases—hence his annoyance at Jerry kissing Mary's hand ('This is nice goin's on in front of her father! ... Chiselurs don't care a damn now about their parents, they're bringin' their fathers' grey hairs down with sorra to the grave, an' laughin' at it, laughin' at it'). When he learns that Mary is pregnant, he plays the outraged father with 'When I'm done with her she'll be the sorry girl', though Juno questions his right to the rôle with 'your fatherly care never throubled the poor girl'. Captain Boyle's inadequacy as a father—his inability or unwillingness to earn for them, to protect them, or even to be loyal to them, is the cause of their scornful and diminishing attitude towards him. His constant cry is 'I've some spirit left in me still'; from his point of view he is being cheated of his position as head of the family, although he is incapable of assuming it.

His failure to his family lies in his detachment. He is not there to give moral support for the news of Johnny's death, to stop the furniture being taken away, or for any other crisis. His worst material crime is in 'cheatin'' the money and using it for himself, running them into further debt after he knows the will to be invalid; in Johnny's words 'you borreyed money from everybody to fill yourself with beer ... I'll tell you what I think of you, father an' all as you are'. He is selfish in all ways. His true grudge about Mary's pregnancy is not for her but for himself: 'That's th' father of Mary Boyle that had th' kid be th' swank she used to go with'. He resents Juno's standing up for Mary: 'Gwan, take her part agen her father'. His unfeeling threat 'Ay, she'll leave this place, an' quick too', provokes Juno's ultimatum 'if Mary goes, I'll go with her'; he connives at his own desertion: 'Well, go with her. Well, go ... I lived before I seen yous, an' I can live when yous are gone'. He withdraws to his own milieu, to Joxer and the pub, and when he comes back drunk he is concerned not with his family's disappearance but with inane generalities about Ireland and the world: 'The counthry'll have to steady itself ... th' whole worl's in a terrible state o' chassis'. It is only when the legacy brings him the position of breadwinner that he draws closer to his family and seems temporarily to be its head: 'I'm masther now'. He and Juno do not fight so much. He calls them all to order, 'peremptorily' but amiably. But the rest of the time he lives in fantasy and drunkenness, both ways of escaping from reality.

Before he enters, we hear about him 'struttin' about like a paycock'. For if Juno is Queen of the Gods, Captain Boyle is clearly not her divine husband Jupiter; nor is he her companion peacock always by her side to do her bidding, his hundred eyes wide open, his nickname 'the all-seeing'—for Captain Boyle is blind to most things. He is drawn from a different legend, that of the jay which decked itself in peacock's feathers to look grand and became an object of ridicule. In Act I he looks grand only in his imagination; in Act II he is resplendent in plumage borrowed 'on credit'. In Act III he is stripped of his finery more painfully and thoroughly than he realises, anaesthetised as he is by alcohol.

He is a scrounger, lazy, 'hates to be assed to stir'; he lies: 'for the last three weeks I haven't tasted a dhrop of intoxicatin' liquor'. He is hasty—about Jerry as one of 'a pack o' spies, pimps and informers', or about Juno: 'I'm not goin' to do only what she damn well likes'. His views on the Church, changing with his wealth, demonstrate his hypocrisy; the variability of his reactions is a recurring joke, as when he says scathingly of his cousin 'is it that prognosticator an' procrastinator? ... sorra many'll go into mournin' for him', and a moment later 'we'll have to go into mournin' at wanst ... I never expected that poor Bill ud die so sudden'. 'You can't believe a word that comes out o' your mouth' says Joxer; this is so, yet, in a sense, Captain Boyle only exists through his words. His seafaring tales are more than mere anecdotes. They are his personality, carefully cultivated, and gaining from the fact that we know and he knows and the people listening to him know that they are fictitious. His whole self goes into the building up of a fictional self: 'Captain Boyle is Captain Boyle'—which of course he is not. This fantasy figure is constructed with elaborate rhetoric: 'I ofen looked up at the sky an' assed meself the question—what is the stars, what is the stars? ... An' then I'd have another look, an' I'd ass meself—what is the moon?'; he needs the accompaniment of Joxer's Hamlet-like 'Ah, that's the question, that's the question'.

Captain Boyle's friendship with Joxer is founded on his need for an audience and egger-on, whose services he pays for in money or sausage-gravy. The relationship fluctuates; at first they are 'butties' united against Juno, but when he thinks he is rich, Captain Boyle says the fatal words 'I'm done with Joxer' and turns to his wife 'O, me darlin' Juno, I will be thrue to thee ... I'm a new man from this out'. But he cannot be a new man, and he needs Joxer. His very next words, at the beginning of Act II are 'Come along, Joxer, me son, come along', and throughout this act they seem friendly. But although the Captain shows Joxer in public for the first time at the party and introduces him with 'the two of us was often in a tight corner', the balance has changed. Boyle is patronising, irritable, corrects him about history, about the priests, about his song: 'I hate to see fellas thryin' to do what they're not able to do'. And although Joxer applauds his verses with 'a daarlin' poem', the idea of maudlin friendship in them is a satiric comment on their own disloyal one. In Act III the disintegration of the Boyle circle is partially seen in Joxer's betrayal of Captain Boyle, by his stealing from him, helping Nugent to outwit him, and crossquestioning him about the will's failure. Joxer justifies himself by saying that Boyle has been 'goin' about like a mastherpiece of the Free State counthry', forgetting his friends and forgetting God. It is not clear whether Boyle has been forgetting God more than usual; his friends have certainly not been forgotten as he lashed out in drink and parties.

Captain Boyle's friendships are seen by his family as degrading. Juno thinks that Bentham would have been right in 'fightin' shy of people like that Joxer fella an' that oul' Madigan wan—nice sort o' people for your father to inthroduce to a man like Mr Bentham'. Johnny detests the friendship: 'Joxer an' you at it agen?—when are you goin' to have a little respect for yourself, an' not be always makin' a show of us all?' But Captain Boyle thinks it is his family which shames him in front of Joxer—'A pretty show I'll be to Joxer an' to that oul' wan, Madigan'. At the core of his friendship with Joxer is fantasy; when they are together they need not be aware of anything outside themselves except as grist to their verbal mill. This escapism, seen also in his drunkenness, is Captain Boyle's main weakness. Neither poverty nor riches, danger nor peace, can make him interested in, or even aware of, what is going on in his country. He is callous: 'if they want to be soldiers ... there's no use o' them squealin'. He is politically detached: 'We've nothin' to do with these things, one way or t'other. That's the government's business, an' let them do what we're paying' them for doin''. O'Casey is sniping at the lackadaisical attitude of the Irishman in the street; even if released from his poverty like the Captain, he is indifferent to the affairs of his country: 'that's enough about them things; they don't affect us, an' we needn't give a damn'.

## Mary

O'Casey's stage directions describe Mary as being driven by two forces, one backward (her environment and the circumstances of her life) and one forward (the influence of the books she had read). The backward force wins; the progression we see is from a positive, independent girl with 'principles' to a passive, dependent, sentimental one. She keeps her dignity but loses her spirit. When her mother makes her plans for the future of the baby, Mary neither assents nor enthuses; she merely makes the sentimental, conventional comment, 'my poor little child that'll have no father'.

But the Mary we meet at the beginning of the play is a staunch trade unionist; her Labour jargon comes easy and militant: 'The hour is past now when we'll ask the employers' permission to wear what we like', 'a principle's a principle'. Her principles are not empty catchphrases. She has 'walked out' on strike for Jennie Claffey, and she believes in solidarity: 'What's the use of belongin' to a Trades Union if you won't stand up for your principles? Why did they sack her? It was a clear case of victimisation'. Although her stance on Labour and other matters is the same as Jerry's, her attitude to him is fiercely independent: 'I want to be by myself'; 'let me go or I'll scream'. The reading by which she tries to lift herself above her environment, and which infuriates her father, is of unromantic, realist plays by Ibsen; plays whose characters must escape convention, face pain, and pursue their individuality. But the Mary we see at the end of the play is conventional. Her love for Bentham is romantic: 'I love him with all my heart and soul'. She thinks he is not the man Jerry is, but 'the best man for a woman is the one for whom she has the most love, and Charlie had it all'. This story book romance is no force pushing her forward; it is Bentham who drags her down, not 'the circumstances of her life'. If Jerry represents intellectual Labour emancipation, Bentham represents worldly status. His 'intellectuality', if any, is only that of a schoolteacher, his 'manners' and apparent worldly wisdom are superficial. Bentham's cowardice in running away rather than admit his error over the will lets Mary down as gravely as if he were a callous seducer; she has been caught with a baby in the eternal female trap.

Mary resembles her mother in many small ways. She is a hard worker, independent and sharp-tongued, yet deferential to Bentham like her mother; she likes dressing up with ribbons and silk stockings as Juno likes buying luxuries when she can. She also has some of Juno's maternal instincts; she offers small comforts to Mrs Tancred and is concerned about Johnny when he sees his ghostly vision. By the end of the play she is protective and comforting to her mother—'Oh mother, mother, me poor darlin' mother'.

Her character develops in dignity and in clearsightedness, reflected in her remarks to Jerry when he fails her after his declarations of undying love. The simplicity of her 'Yes, Jerry, as you say, I have fallen as low as that' and her calm 'Let us say no more' are in dignified contrast to his passionate utterances and his humiliating 'have you fallen as low as that?'. Now she sees him clearly, and sheds her illusions that he is more of a man than Bentham or her brother or father. Now she sees that his vaunted humanity is just as narrow as the humanity of the others. This is her great disillusionment; he has let her down as much as Bentham; his reaction to her pregnancy is as convential and callous as Jerry's or Captain Boyle's. What she sees in his verses is disharmony and spoiling—of herself, of Ireland and of humanity.

## Johnny

In Johnny's mutilated body we see the futility of heroism. It has lost him his only birthright, the ability to work. He has undoubtedly behaved heroically by the light of the romance that had already grown up around the heroes of the 1916 Rising, yet he has betrayed his comrade Tancred. This betrayal is never explained: if it was pure treachery, it is a commentary on the fleeting quality of human heroism; if it was the result of some convolution of his 'principles' it accentuates the horror of civil war, Irishman against Irishman, neighbour against neighbour, friend against friend.

Johnny is certainly no hero by the time the play takes place: he is a self-pitying coward, who betrays his fear at every move, and flinches at every knock. He is edgy, bad-tempered, intolerant of everyone. His reactions to the other characters show the disintegration, through the three acts, of a personality under intolerable strain. Behind this iras- cibility hides a pitiable child, glimpsed in his faith in the protection of his mother and of the Virgin Mary. The duality of his character is established early; in the stage directions he is thin, delicate, pale and drawn, missing an arm and limping; he has evidently gone through a rough time and has 'a tremulous look of indefinite fear in his eyes'. But for Mary he is a man of steel: 'He stuck to his principles, an' no matther how you may argue, ma, a principle's a principle'. On the one hand we see the fretful child 'I won't stop here be meself!'—on the other he sets himself up as a strong man: 'I'd do it agen ma, I'd do it agen; for a principle's a principle'. But his principles are mere jingo jargon: 'Ireland only half free'll never be at peace while she has a son left to pull a trigger'. This bloodthirstiness is now only superficial—he cannot bear even to hear about killing: 'quit that readin' for God's sake ... It'll soon be that none of you'll read anythin' that's not about butcherin''; 'Is there nothin' betther to be talkin' about but the killin' o' people?'

In his desire to evade the punishment for his crime, Johnny adds to the claustrophobic atmosphere of the house. To him, the will means 'We'll be able to get out o' this place now, an' go somewhere we're not known'. He has the prevalent escapism: 'I wish to God a bullet or a bomb had whipped me ou' o' this long ago'; and the prevalent selfishness: 'Not one o' yous have any thought for me'. He becomes more and more aggressive as the pursuit draws closer and the pressure builds up. He accuses the rest of the family of shaming him, his father for being friendly with Joxer, Mary for 'burnin' to tell everyone of the shame you've brought on us'. He attacks his father for running them into debt: 'Take care somebody doesn't lay his han's on you'; Juno for giving way to Boyle over money; and Mary, most callously: 'She should be dhriven out o' th' house she's brought disgrace on'.

His pathetic impotence is shown when he cannot even try to stop the furniture men removing their possessions, but has to send for the father he has just been reviling. For Johnny has been negated and given the 'finishin' touch' when he lost his arm: 'them's the only sort o' principles that's any good to a workin' man'. His body is recognisable in the end, ironically, only by the lack of that arm. Johnny's disintegration is echoed in a loss of his individuality. While Mrs Tancred's entrance humanises her son from an abstract figure to a real person, the arrival of the Mobilizer transforms Johnny from the son and brother we have met into the figure of a soldier. He is a part of a Battalion, not as Johnny but as 'Quarther-Masther Boyle', and ought to have been responsible to it. His guilt and responsibility are confirmed by the Irregulars. He has actively betrayed Tancred: 'You gave him away to the gang that sent him to his grave'.

Faced with the summons to answer for his action, he crumbles: he is 'not well', he 'won't go', he cringes and pleads 'haven't I done enough for Ireland', far from the bravado of 'I'd do it agen, ma'. His vision of Tancred's body has already revealed his defensiveness ('Oh, why did he look at me like that . . . it wasn't my fault that he was done in') and his cowardice ('keep him away from me'). Above all it has shown his reliance on the outer forms of religion without any inner grace. He thinks that a votive light, a picture, a few snatches of prayer, can protect him from the consequences of his sin. It is ironic that the very statue and light that he relies on for protection turn into a vision of his sin, the scarlet Sacred Heart into the bloody breast of Tancred. Our pity for Johnny is not for a noble character with a fatal flaw, but for a fallible one, inextricably caught up in and corrupted by a system not devised by himself. He represents the maimed youth of Ireland, cheated of their right to live and work sensibly by the follies of senseless heroics and civil war.

## Joxer

Unlike his friend Captain Boyle, Joxer is no peacock. He does not seek grandeur; he is content to camouflage himself, to let Captain Boyle do the bragging to his echo. His true instinct is for self-preservation, evident when he goes onto the roof to escape Juno or refuses to look out of the window for fear of 'a bullet in the kisser'. This is the motive behind his sycophantic words and 'ingratiating' mannerisms. He is a scrounger, who stands by and waits his chance of a sausage, five shillings, or a drink.

As a yes-man, he has elaborate ways of agreeing: 'you could sing that if you had an air to it'. He may expand Boyle's statement while laying claim to it—'You're afther takin' the word out o' me mouth—afther all, a Christian's natural, but he's unnatural'; and he can echo conflicting statements with the same conviction—Boyle's anti-clerical 'I never like to be beholden to any o' the clergy' with 'it's dangerous, right enough', and his pro-clerical 'I don't like anyone to talk disrespectful of Father Farrell' with 'I wouldn't let a word be said agen Father Farrell—the heart o' the rowl, that's what he is'. His remarks are unoriginal compared with those of Captain Boyle, who deflates him whenever he volunteers an opinion of his own; he is allowed to take the initiative in criticising Juno: 'It's a terrible thing to be tied to a woman that's always grousin'. I don't know how you stick it—it ud put years on me'. As well as applauding with easy 'daarlin''s, his task is to feed Captain Boyle with his seafaring stories as a straight man might feed a comedian: 'God be with the young days when you were steppin' the deck of a manly ship'.

He is stung into revealing the malevolence of his true feelings when Captain Boyle disowns him—'Joxer out on the roof with the win' blowin' through him was nothin' to you an' your frien' with the collar an' tie'. His comradeship evaporates and he mocks the very story he has been abetting—'I was dhreamin' I was standin' on the bridge of a ship ... an' sayin', what is the stars, what is the stars?'. He betrays him: 'I have to laugh every time I look at the deep-sea sailor; an' a row on a river ud make him sea-sick!' And he even gives away Captain Boyle's real views on work, so carefully concealed by the pains in his legs: 'Lookin' for work, an' prayin' to God he won't get it'. This is the first time we see him not sycophantic to Captain Boyle; it gives Juno the opportunity to say 'maybe now you see yourself the kind he is' and presages his later hostility.

Back in favour with the now 'rich' Captain Boyle, Joxer gives renewed avowals of the friendship we know to be empty: 'me for you an' you for me'. But in Act III he becomes sinister and menacing. Stealing stout and letting the theft be put down to Nugent is normal scrounging; but he actively hounds his friend, conspires with Nugent against him, and asserts his superiority: 'It's very seldom he escapes me'. He cross-questions Boyle relentlessly about the will, knowing the answers already—'She must ha' heard some rumour or other that you weren't going' to get th' money . . . must be somethin' behind it . . . Did he hear anythin' . . . about you not gettin' the money?' In a travesty of their friendly badinage, they hotly debate 'who's a twisther?', and Joxer finally calls him 'Jacky Boyle, Esquire, infernal rogue an' damned liar'. He is ready later to go drinking with him, to spend all but his last sixpence and to echo his last drunken sentiments with snatches of song; but we know how disloyal his friendship is.

Like Mary and Jerry, Joxer has his own jargon—his is made up of ill-digested and ill-remembered scraps of nineteenth-century 'culture'—parlour poetry and song, saws and proverbs. His appearance with Captain Boyle in the last few moments of the play is the apotheosis of this scrap-collecting from many sources. He often sings about bravery—'How can a man die betther', 'Let me like a soldier fall, me breast expandin' to the ball'. Anything he says is debased into a cliché in his mouth; he parrots, but does not reflect on, many sayings that are ironic commentaries on the play—'where ignorance's bliss, 'tis folly to be wise'. His quotation of 'Man's inhumanity to man makes countless thousands mourn' echoes the true meaning of the play and states Mary's sincere philosophy in a few banal, over-familiar and unmeant words. He expresses the very worst of sentimental jingo—'this is my own, my native land', in the mouth of one who cares nothing for his country.

Juno sees him as corrupting Captain Boyle. But Joxer is only 'ready'; it is Boyle's own indolence and drunkenness that seeks him out. When called he is always at hand—'say the word, an' I'll be with you, like a bird'. His is recalled as a necessary part of Captain Boyle's backsliding, boasting and drinking. He mirrors the worst side of Boyle by following and echoing him—but he is in fact more astute than Boyle. He represents the worst of the Irish, devious and dishonest yet claiming good fellowship and patriotism. 'Chains an' slaveree . . . that's a daaar-lin' motto!' is the essence of his bondage to poverty and ignorance.

## Bentham

Charlie Bentham acts as a catalyst in the play. First, he is the agent of the will—bearer, writer and reader of that miraculous document which seems to be the solution of the Boyle's material problems. Second, he is the precipitator of Johnny's hysterical 'vision'. Third, he acts on Mary's general dissatisfaction with her lot to cause her downfall. He appears from outside the Boyles' circle to alienate her from Jerry, with whom she had apparently shared happy loving hours until she 'clicked' with this 'thin, lanky strip of a Micky Dazzler'. It is significant that Bentham never has a loving scene with Mary in the play as Jerry does; her affair with him seems merely another of the characters' attempts to escape their circumstances. Mary's motives are not purely materialistic; Jerry too can lift her out of 'all this' when he gets his salary of £350 a year. But Bentham represents a gentility in elegant contrast with Jerry's down-to-earth Labour interests. He will lift her out of her class with politeness and small-talk: 'Juno! what an interesting name!', 'it's just as you were saying', 'how pretty you're looking', 'we won't be long away, Mrs Boyle'. Mary never suggests that he is morally superior to Jerry: 'I often thought to myself that he wasn't the man poor Jerry was, but I couldn't help loving him, all the same'. He does not appear to have loved her with any integrity; her pregnancy makes his absence a betrayal, and calls forth Juno's 'Oh, is there not even a middlin' honest man left in the world?' He is not man enough to face his mistake in drawing up the will; he explains neither to Boyle nor to Mary, preferring to give the impression that he has left because they are not good enough for him.

Bentham's distinguishing features are external: yellow gloves, smart clothes, a walking stick. His conversational accessories are just as glaring and vulgar. His theosophy is one manifestation of this vulgarity. In his autobiography, O'Casey describes the poet AE, a leading theosophist, as 'Dublin's Glittering Guy', mocking the superficiality of his art and of his spiritualism. Bentham's conversation glitters in the same empty way with the stock-in-trade of cheap 'religion': Vedas, Yogi and supernatural theories to blind us with science, as they blind Johnny into 'seeing things'. Bentham's belief in the Universal Life-Breath looks flimsy set against his attitude to the Republicans, callously voiced directly after Mrs Tancred's appearance: 'the only way to deal with a mad dog is to destroy him'. 'His Majesty Bentham', as Captain Boyle calls him sarcastically, has a high opinion of himself, and is deferred to by all including Mary and Juno; but the elegant exterior hides the fool, the coward and the abandoning lover, the epitome of man's inhumanity to woman. It is not the Boyles who are 'not good enough' for Bentham; it is he who has failed them. Indeed, they are worse off after his apparently benevolent interventions than if he had never appeared.

## Jerry

Jerry acts as a foil for Mary, showing her at her most confident and at her most vulnerable. He is also the personification of the Labour movement, and O'Casey gives us clear instructions of how we should see him. Whereas he sees himself as a worthy member of his trade union, almost certain of becoming its secretary, 'popular with all the men an' a good speaker', to O'Casey he typifies one of the new suspect leaders of the Labour movement in 1922. He is clever enough to shape the mass of his more ignorant associates into a power, but not clever enough to 'broaden that power for the benefit of all'. He has the knowledge, the energy and the rhetoric to lead his co-workers, but not the wider compassion nor the wider understanding to see the need for a world Labour movement rather than a narrowly Irish one: he is a Connolly rather than a Larkin. We see Jerry's Labour concern to find Captain Boyle a job, a concern comically doomed to fail in the face of the Captain's determination not to work. He seems a good, practical man lacking only the higher vision. What we hear about him from others confirms his worthiness: 'We all know Devine knows a little more than the rest of us ... he's a good boy, sober, able to talk an' all that', says the Captain, not seeing these as desirable qualities, 'I never heard him usin' a curse; I don't believe he was ever dhrunk in his life'. Contrasted with Bentham, he is always the worker, Bentham the Micky-Dazzler—'Jerry believin' in nothin', an' Bentham believin' in everythin'. One that says all is God an' no man; an' th' other (Jerry) that says all is man an' no God'. Until his last scene with Mary he seems a man of true worth; it is one of the tragedies of the play that his humanity and compassion prove just as empty as Bentham's and everybody else's.

His first love scene with Mary has two values: its face value in which he seems the worthy lover scorned, and its ironic aspect in hindsight when we look back on his declarations of eternal love from his rejection of her in Act III. He seems a sympathetic character, by turns sad, pleading, firm and lyrical. But the ironic foreshadowing of their last meeting in Act III in which he rejects her for being pregnant is always present: 'No matther what happens, you'll always be the same to me'.

Ironically, all the nobility and 'humanity' of Jerry's character lead up to his denial of Mary in the third act. He is forgiving—as far as he goes. The 'everything' that he thinks Juno has told him can be encompassed by his love, now 'greater and deeper than ever'; they are young enough to be able to forget that Mary once left him for Bentham. As he pleads for her love he invokes the idea of Labour on his side. 'With Labour, Mary, humanity is above everything; we are the Leaders in the fight for a new life'. This crescendo of passion is let down at its peak. From what we know of Jerry so far, this is not expected. He could well have had a humanitarian concern for her, or have been above conventional morals as he is 'above' conventional religion. But his words are as conventional as they are scornful: 'have you fallen as low as that?' This is a cruel blow; and although he partially retracts his scorn with 'I didn't mean it that way, Mary', his excuses are feeble; it has come on him unexpectedly; he is 'sorry'. Another 'principle' in the play has proved unworkable in practice. He does not remember the verses from his lecture—nor does he speak after Mary has recited them. He is now unwilling to face the ugliness and discord which the poem states man has brought to Nature's order. In Jerry's lecture he would have been on the side of 'humanity'; in practice he is himself an example of cruelty. His insufficiency in his love for Mary is closely linked with his insufficiency in Labour and in the fight for humanity; he lacks compassion and fails Mary as conclusively as her father, brother and Bentham do.

## Mrs Tancred

Mrs Tancred is a reflection of Juno's later character as a bereaved mother, and her story is a dramatic parallel to Juno's, adding poignancy to the fate that we sense is creeping up on her.

She is a symbol of suffering womanhood but she is also a real person; in fact her human reality is necessary to counterbalance her abstract significance. Until her entrance her son's death has seemed impersonal, a statistic among the war casualty lists, a column in the newspaper. She establishes the human as opposed to the political significance of his death, the supposed nobility of which is nothing to her maternal grief—'What's the pains I suffered bringin' him into the world to carry him to his cradle, to the pains I'm sufferin' now, carryin' him out o' the world to bring him to his grave!' This is the elemental grief of any mother whose only child dies before her: 'I seen the first of him an' I'll see the last of him'. She moves between the personal and the general, placing herself consciously in a symbolic position opposite Mrs Manning, the other bereaved mother, 'one on each side of a scales o' sorra'. It is she who makes the poetic expression of the play's message: the dead boys are mothers' sons, not Diehards and Freestaters, and she prays that all eyes may be opened to this fact: 'Sacred Heart of the Crucified Jesus, take away our hearts o' stone ... an' give us hearts o' flesh! Take away this murdherin' hate ... an' give us Thine own eternal love'.

We see Mrs Tancred through Juno's eyes at two levels, first as the abstract 'Diehard Mother' who by allowing her house to be used has brought her fate on herself and 'deserves all she got'. Second, when Juno too is a victim, she sees her as a sister. With their 'two dear darlin' sons' dead, Juno in her turn becomes the counterbalance to Mrs Tancred on their formal scales of suffering, and echoing her key prayer, reaffirms the plays' humanitarian message; so that the one-time collaborator, Mrs Tancred, serves a pacifist purpose.

## Needle Nugent

Needle Nugent is always closely linked to the theme of money. He is even more self-interested than Maisie Madigan; like her his friendship is in direct proportion to the Boyles' supposed richness. He confirms that Captain Boyle is not going to get his money, and, worse from the point of view of his creditors, that he has known this for a long time. Nugent is the herald of Boyle's downfall: 'he's not goin' to throw his weight about in the suit I made for him much longer'. He is the first to start denuding Boyle of his borrowed plumes, with 'I like your damn cheek . . . what do I care what you dhress yourself in!'

He represents the clichés of Irish nationalism: 'Have none of yous any respect for the Irish people's National regard for the dead?'; to O'Casey as to Juno the opposite of true humanity, regard for the living. To Maisie Madigan his hypocrisy is even more blatant; he is one of those making money from both sides, 'attendin' Republican funerals in the day, an' stoppin' up half the night makin' suits for the Civic Guards', the new Irish police who are fighting them. Nugent is an ordinary Dubliner on the make, uncommitted to the Boyles, with the jingoistic phrases of Irish brotherhood ready to his lips and far from his heart.

## Mrs Madigan

Maisie Madigan has three very practical uses in the play. First, in her capacity of credit-raiser and purveyor of goods, she provides the outward results of the legacy without its having to be received by the Boyles. Second, in direct contrast, she is an agent of their bankruptcy, coming in to claim her money and taking away the gramophone. Third, she provides light relief and dramatic anti-climax at several crucial points. After Johnny's hysterical vision of Tancred's bloody 'ghost', her arrival for the party makes an abrupt and bathetic change of mood. Her chatter and vulgar *bonhomie* are in powerful contrast to the funeral and Mrs Tancred's grief, and after Mrs Tancred's appearance she is quick to change the mood again by calling for Captain Boyle's song.

Like Needle Nugent she is on the make, her friendship dependent on the Boyles' money. But there is more room for her character to develop. The stage directions have her 'ignorant, vulgar and forward, but her heart is generous withal'. We see her generosity in small matters like getting a shawl for Mrs Tancred and later supporting Juno in her grief. Yet she is determined to strip the Boyles of their wealth and get more than her money's worth from them. Ironically, as she has assisted in stripping the Boyles, it is she who brings the news of their greatest loss—that of their son. The relationship of her character to Juno's is complex. Maisie's corresponds to the frivolous side of Juno—the side that buys the gramophone. Juno's feeling that Bentham has left because he was 'fightin' shy' of her and Joxer reflects her uneasiness that the Boyles themselves are not good enough for him. Maisie also voices Juno's own scorn for Captain Boyle, echoing Juno's Paycock simile, and threatening to 'pull some o' th' gorgeous feathers' out of his tail. Her fury as she tries to shake the money out of Captain Boyle is a wry twist of his original description of her as 'an oul' back-parlour neighbour, that, if she could help it at all, ud never see a body shuk (shook)', that is, short of money. She has Juno's sharp tongue, too, inveighing against Needle Nugent and against the police ('You're the same as yous were undher the British Government—never where yous are wanted').

Maisie Madigan's strange vulgar lyricism is her most distinctive feature. Odd moments of her slum life have been snatched in the country and she expresses her romantic ideas in blossoms, nightingales at mating time and other country clichés: she is a parody of the lovers she coyly nudges. Her romantic picture of herself is always in the act of singing and her emotions are intermingled with the cheap or pretentious sentiment of her songs.

# Language

## The power of the word

Much of the 'realism' of *Juno and the Paycock* comes from its accuracy of speech. Its Dublin intonations unerringly establish a reality of setting and of character. Even those features which have an expressly dramatic purpose, like repetition, rhetoric, lyrical or biblical passages, fall easily on the ear in natural spoken rhythms. Language plays a large part in the swift changes of pace and mood characteristic of the play, and strengthens both its tragedy and its comedy. Effects can range from simple funny mispronunciation to the wild full-blown rhetoric of Captain

Boyle; from the casual lyricism of Maisie Madigan's reminiscences to Mrs Tancred's bitter balanced elegy for her son, all against a general background of quickwitted, idiomatic repartee, full of imagery and fantasy.

The power of the word is acknowledged in the play, by allusions like Jerry's poignant 'you hardly speak to me, an' then only a word with the face o' bittherness on it'. The characters manipulate their own speech for effect; Captain Boyle's call for a drink, 'A wet—a jar—a boul!', prompts Juno's 'Jack, you're speakin' to Mr Bentham, an' not to Joxer', an acknowledgment that he varies his utterance to his audience. He himself explains that he knows the correct form, but the wrong one sounds better in his story—'it blowed an' blowed—blew is the right word, Joxer, but blowed is what the sailors use'. This conscious choice of words is evident in the use of catchphrases like Joxer's 'a darlin' buk, a daarlin' buk'—like a personal 'signature tune' or slogan.

## Dialect

Such catchphrases give an individual flavour to each person's speech; there are also individual mispronunciations caused by failure to grasp words properly, like Captain Boyle's 'chassis', 'dockyment' or 'pereeogative'. But there are numerous more subtle variations of the language. Its principal colouring comes from the regional Irish dialect and vocabulary, faithfully produced, slang phrases, mistakes in English grammar, and English forms that are direct renderings of Irish phrases.

Practically every speech in the play contains examples of Dublin dialect mispronunciation. Typical samples include vowel sounds distorted and spelt phonetically: *wan, wance, at wanst* (for *one, once, at once*); *yis* (*yes*); *at our ayse, ayther, tay* (*at our ease, either, tea*); *me, be, meself* (*may, by, myself*); *kem, ketch* (*came, catch*); *oul', houl'* (*old, hold*); *swally, folley* (*swallow, follow*). Consonants are often thickened—*misundherstand, dhrink, afther, thrap, wather*; *bud* for *but*. Many final consonants are omitted—*han'* for *hand, tole* for *told, ass* for *ask, ou' o'* for *out of, I'd ha'* for *I'd have*, and particularly final 'g' in words ending with -*ing*—*comin', mournin', livin'*. There is a great deal of elision—*t'England, g' win* for *go in, gwan* for *go on* and *th'* for *the* before vowels or consonants—*th' oul, th' kid*. Second person pronouns are typically Irish *yez, yous* and *ye* for *you*.

Specially Anglo-Irish vocabulary includes *collogin'* for *discussing, sorra many* for *not many, lashin's o' time* for *a lot of time, chiselurs* for *children, gawkin'* for *staring, banjax* for *mess, butty* for *friend, a ball o' malt* for *a glass of whiskey, me last juice* for *my last penny*.

Merging with these are contemporary slang—*a Micky Dazzler, climb up my back, right as the mail, Jack-actin'*, and addresses like *me boyo, me buck*. Mistakes in English grammar include phrases like *I'm terrible late, more comfortabler, riz* for *rose*. Although there is no Irish language in the play exept for the Captain's mistaken *guh sayeree jeea ayera, God save Ireland* , which he confuses with *rest in peace* (with an equally mistaken idea that Saint Patrick and Saint Brigid spoke Irish not Latin), there is a particularly faithful reproduction of Irish rhythms and intonations. The most striking examples of this are unusual English forms that are direct renderings of Irish phrases; they are apparent in the alien syntax: *and I afther going', an' they starvin', an' we singin'; any man havin' the like of them pains id be down an' out; do you want e'er a sewin' machine; afther puttin' the heart across me; amn't I nicely handicapped with the lot of you?* This Irish formation of otherwise English sentences is noticeable in frequent inversion: *it's a docthor you should have been; it's yourself that has yourself the way y'are'; it's not because he was commandant of the Battalion that I was Quarther-masther of, that we were friends.*

## Characterisation through speech

O'Casey differentiates between his characters' speech; Bentham's genteel correctness, 'please don't put youself to any trouble, Mrs Boyle—I'm quite all right here, thank you' or 'It was simply due to an overwrought imagination—we all get that way at times', is quite unlike Maisie Madigan's vulgar 'You're goin' to get as nice a bit o' skirt in Mary, there, as ever you seen in your puff'. We have seen that characters sometimes consciously manipulate the degree of dialect in their speech, but there are also unconscious variations. Mary's speech, like her manners, is subject to the opposing forces of literature and environment, so that at times she speaks standard English: 'Now you know all, Jerry, now you know all', or 'there's no necessity, really, mother to go to the doctor; nothing serious is wrong with me—I'm run down and disappointed, that's all'. But when we first meet her, she speaks broadly—'out beyant Finglas he was found . . . seven wounds he had—one entherin' the neck . . . another in the left breast penethratin' the heart', where the consonants are thickened and she uses inversion. When she is alarmed she speaks even more broadly—'Mother o' God, he made me heart lep!' Such contrasts are used for comedy. Joxer's natural speech is flat Dublin, 'g'wan in at wanst, man, an' get it off him, an' don't be a fool', against which his 'borrowings' sit strangely: 'an honest man's the noblest work o' God'; 'where ignorance's bliss 'tis folly to be wise'.

## Repetition

Most of the speakers use repetition, often for emphasis, or as a substitute for articulate development of a statement. It is used particularly at times of stress, and for comic effects either in exaggeration or in quick repartee.

Johnny, who is under constant strain, consistently repeats his phrases: 'I can rest nowhere, nowhere, nowhere'; 'let me alone, let me alone, let me alone', 'I won't hole me tongue, I won't hole me tongue'; 'I'll not be quiet, I'll not be quiet', 'I'd do it agen, ma, I'd do it agen', and, under extreme stress, 'Haven't I done enough for Ireland?' twice. He and Mary also repeat their jargon: 'A principle's a principle'. Juno, when very worried, says 'you're not serious Jack' twice, 'I don't believe it' three times.

When used for comic effect, the repetition is often in direct proportion to the falsity of the statement, like Captain Boyle's 'I'm a man of spirit' all through Act I, or Joxer's 'an' we kem out of it flyin', Captain, we kem out of it flyin''. When Captain Boyle is blustering about Bentham he repeats threats we know he will never carry out: 'I'll folly him' and 'he'll marry her, he'll have to marry her'. The catchphrases such as Joxer's 'daarlin'' and Boyle's 'prognosticator and procrastinator' have a cumulatively funny effect through repetition, and phrases are played with in different tones in different scenes. 'What is the stars' appears first in Boyle's reminiscences, and is repeated by Joxer first sycophant-ically and later mockingly. Captain Boyle's 'the whole worl's in a terrible state o' chassis' is repeated many times. Its effect is usually funny, as when he objects to Jerry kissing Mary, or uses it continually about world affairs ('I was just tellin' Mr Bentham . . .'); but at the end of the play it is repeated one last time for an ironically tragic effect.

Repetition is also used from person to person for cross-talk: Captain Boyle: 'Are you never goin' to give us a rest?' Mrs Boyle 'Oh, you're never tired o' lookin' for a rest', or Captain Boyle: 'D'ye want to dhrive me out o' the house?' Mrs Boyle: 'It ud be easier to dhrive you out o' the house than to dhrive you into a job', and the exchanges between Captain Boyle and Joxer: 'don't be a twisther.' 'Who's a twisther?' . . . 'You never twisted yourself . . .' 'Did you ever know me to twist; did you ever know me to twist?' 'Did you ever do anythin' else?'. Phrases repeated from person to person can also mark tragedy. Johnny's repe-tition of the 'Hail Mary' reminds us of Tancred's funeral, and the dramatic axis of the play is Juno's repetition of Mrs Tancred's elegy for her son.

## Balance

Mrs Tancred's lament is the most remarkable example of balance in the play: 'Ah, what's the *pains* I *suffered bringin'* him *into the world* to *carry* him to his *cradle*, to the *pains* I'm *sufferin'* now, *carryin'* him *out o' the world* to *bring* him to his *grave'*. Here *pains* is the constant. Past and present are contrasted in *suffered* and *suffering*, direction in *into the world* and *out o' the world*; *bringin' him ... to carry him* inverted to *carryin' him ... to bring him*; the resolution of the balance is in the opposition of *cradle* and *grave*. Juno's echo is even more poignantly addressed to Johnny in the first person singular: 'bringin' you into the world to carry you to your cradle'. Mrs Tancred, echoed by Juno, also contrasts and balances 'hearts o' stone' with 'hearts o' flesh', 'murdherin' hate' with 'eternal love', and 'I seen the first of him' with 'I'll see the last of him'. She opposes the neighbours' 'he died a noble death an' we'll bury him like a king' with a balance between death and life, king and pauper, in 'an' I'll go on livin' like a pauper'. This balance can occur at less tragic times too: the CID raided 'either when th' sun was risin' or when th' sun was settin'', or 'Jerry believin' in nothin' an' Bentham believin' in everythin'. One that says all is God an' no man; an' th'other that says all is man an' no God!'

## Lyricism

In Mrs Tancred's speech we recognise, besides her religious imagery, her own poetic lyricism and a heightening of her language. 'Her Freestate soldier son' is not a wholly natural word-order; nor is 'his head, his darlin' head, that I often kissed an' fondled, half hidden in the wather of a runnin' brook'. Her speech is reminiscent of the rhythmic 'keening', half eulogy, half lament, wailed by Irish mourners over the dead: 'Me home is gone now; he was me only child ...' When Jerry remembers his loving times with Mary he is lyrical: 'Have you forgotten, Mary, all the happy evenin' that were as sweet as the scented hawthorn that sheltered the sides o' the road as we sauntered through the country?' So is Maisie Madigan, reminiscing about her 'own man' 'ketchin' hould of a danglin' bramble branch, holdin' clusters of the loveliest flowers you ever seen'—the country images and rhythmic phrases painting a romantic picture for both.

## Rhetoric

Captain Boyle's rhetorical method is to build up and up. He can start with the Gulf of Mexico and proceed by way of fierce winds and himself fixed to the wheel with a marlin-spike to a philosophic question, 'what is the stars?' and carry on even further to 'what is the moon?' He can accumulate question after question in the same way, as in his argument about the priests—'Didn't they prevent the people in '47 from seizin' the corn, an' they starvin'; didn't they down Parnell; didn't they say that hell wasn't hot enough nor eternity long enough to punish the Fenians?' His response to his own rhetorical questions is 'we don't forget, we don't forget them things' and he moves on to a heartrending 'If they've taken everything else from us, Joxer, they've left us our memory', thus running the gamut of patriotic claptrap. Mary's and Johnny's slogans are readymade rhetoric; 'a principle's a principle'. And when Jerry is declaring his love he can sound as if he were addressing a public meeting: 'With Labour, Mary, humanity is above everything; we are the Leaders in the fight for a new life'.

## Imagery

All the characters use a vivid imagery quite casually, whether it be a standard 'you can't get blood out of a turnip' or 'he can't be let go to the fair', or a more individual 'he was off like a redshank'. Juno's is the most striking: 'don't be actin' as if you couldn't pull a wing out of a dead bee'; 'you can skip like a goat into a snug' and even the graphic 'get wan o' the labourers to carry you down in a hod'. Her imagery can be macabre: 'Mrs Tancred's only son gone west with his body made a collandher of'.

# Terms of reference

## Literary references

O'Casey uses his characters' literary allusions to given an extra dimension to what is being said; the effect is usually of irony, either conscious or unconscious on the part of the speaker. Joxer's literary tags may seem a ragbag of rubbish; but many of them embody an ironic truth strictly relevant to the play, although unthinkingly used by him. When Captain Boyle discovers that his bottle of stout has gone, Joxer, who has stolen it, remarks 'Man's inhumanity to man makes countless thousands mourn', a quotation from Robert Burns's 'Man was made to mourn', a large theme applied to a petty object. But on a different level it expresses the whole message of the play, which is a lesson against inhumanity from the military to the personal. For Captain Boyle's cheating and borrowing, he produces 'an honest man's the noblest work o' God', an ironic comment on all the men in the play, for, as Juno asks 'is there not even a middlin' honest man left in th' world?'. Even his reference to 'the cup that cheers but doesn't . . .' from Cowper's 'the cup that cheers but not inebriates' is ironic in this drink-orientated household. Many fleeting references have this ironic idea of contrast—Bentham's reference to 'Homer's glorious story of ancient gods and heroes' contrasts pathetically with Juno's real life. *Willy Reilly and his own Coleen Bawn* is a romantic novel by William Carleton about penal times when Irish Catholics were cruelly oppressed by the English Protestants; a handsome young Catholic elopes with a Protestant heiress. The parallel with an oppressed 1920s Ireland is inevitable—Joxer's mention of it a drink sodden tribute to romantic nationalism. His 'didya ever rade Elizabeth, or Th 'Exile o' Sibayria?' is also ironic; it is a tale of a girl who trekked thousands of miles across frozen Russia to have her father freed from exile, and cuts across the Boyle family where children and parents fail each other, and Mary by the end is a weaker character who needs to be protected and rescued by her mother. Even Captain Boyle's comic confusion of the *Story of Ireland*'s author, M. Sullivan, with the heavyweight champion, J.L. Sullivan, is a comment on his ignorance of Irish history and literature.

The most striking and consistent literary link is with Ibsen, prompted by Mary's books, but relevant to the whole play. Mary's reading is an integral part of her—the force that improves her while her environment degrades her. She is reading, specifically, Ibsen. The three plays mentioned are *A Doll's House*, *Ghosts*, and *The Wild Duck*. But these plays have a much more specific relevance that merely to show that 'where ignorance's bliss 'tis folly to be wise'. They preach liberation from convention, and reinforce O'Casey's message. At the end of *A Doll's House*, Nora, caught in a stifling marriage, leaves her husband's house with a dramatic off-stage slam of the door. Ibsen's message was that marriage is not sacrosanct; it does not make one 'happy ever after'; a man's authority in his home is not meant to stay unchallenged. The comparison with Juno's leaving home and Captain Boyle is unavoidable. Ibsen preaches the right and need of the individual to find out who he or she is. Juno cannot stay in this home with this husband and be the kind of person she really is; the noble and generous person she has developed into in the course of the play. *Ghosts*, too, is about the devitalising effect of dumbly accepting convention. In it, the sins of the fathers are visited upon the children in the shape of heriditary syphilis—much as the Boyle children suffer from inherited poverty, ignorance and degradation. *The Wild Duck* contains a father and son hiding in illusion, and two sensible earth-bound women. Several of its themes can be applies to *Juno and the Paycock*: one cannot be freed from outside, as Juno cannot be freed by the legacy but must liberate herself. Wild ducks degenerate in captivity, as Juno's nobler spirit has in the confines of her marriage. Most people refuse to go on living and face reality once they have been hurt; Juno's willingness to go forward and look after Mary and her child when her husband fails her and her son is killed, shows her to be one of the few with this strength. These plays were much discussed at the time *Juno and the Paycock* was produced; *A Doll's House* had been staged at the Abbey in 1923. O'Casey admired Ibsen's work; both playwrights attack the provincial outlook, the narrow and inhibiting effect of small-town life and the suppression of individual freedom from inside and outside. The parallels with Mary's Ibsen reading add an extra dimension to *Juno and the Paycock*.

## Musical references

The songs in *Juno and the Paycock* are drawn from a variety of sources, from street ballads to grand opera; the majority would have been familiar to Abbey Theatre audiences in florid arrangements for drawing-room recitals—poetry set to music, gems from grand opera and light opera, English, American and Italian. They serve several distinct purposes in the play, and like the literary references they are often overlaid with irony. First, they are outlets for gaiety, a primary human need and right according to O'Casey. Second, they can express a thought that an inarticulate speaker cannot voice in his own words. Third, the choice of song in this play is often escapist—too romantic or grand for its surroundings. Fourth, the text of the song can be in complete opposition to its context in the play. Fifth, and most heavily ironic, some of the songs are commentaries on the nationalist jingo criticised in many other ways in the play.

As an expression of gaiety, the sing-song party is in itself an acknowledgement of release from poverty. A Dublin street ballad like 'If I were a blackbird I'd whistle and sing' expressing love and fidelity, seems a logical choice for such a gathering, as indeed does Captain Boyle's singing of a similar faithful-lover ballad, the American 'when the robins nest agen' as he cooks his sausage contentedly. But even so simple an expression of joy and companionship as a sing-song is in itself ironically set against the background of Tancred's funeral and the singing of the Sacred Heart hymn.

The use of song to express emotion has something sad in it. These people, despite their flood of words, are inarticulate: if they wish to express something they do not necessarily have the right words to hand, so have to use secondhand clichés to express their feelings. Maisie Madigan's memory of herself fifteen years ago—her acquaintance with love is a day in the country, a hackneyed ballad: 'I thought me buzzom was every minute goin' to burst out into a roystherin' song about "The little green leaves that were shakin' in the threes,/The gallivantin' buttherflies, an' buzzin' o' the bees!" '

The operatic arias strike an escapist and fantastic note in the poor surroundings in which they are sung. The song that Maisie Madigan remembers herself singing, 'An' You'll Remember Me', for example, is from Balfe's opera *The Bohemian Girl*: 'There may perhaps in such a scene,/Some recollection be/Of days that have as happy been,/And you'll remember me, and you'll remember me'. The songs Joxer attempts have the same romantic unsuitability to the singer and the surroundings. His sentimental 'shut-eyed wans' are the sort of song that the greatly-lionised Irish tenor John McCormack (1884–1945) was currently popularising on gramophone records, cashing in, many thought, on his Irishness. One is English, 'I have heard the mavis singing' from 'Mary of Argyle' continuing "Twas thy voice, my gentle Mary,/And thy artless, winning smile/That made the world an Eden', a thought too romantic for this far from paradisal place. 'She is far from the land' from Thomas Moore's *Irish Melodies*, is another love-song, that of Sarah Curran and Robert Emmet, the Irish patriot executed in 1803, again over-elevated for the surroundings.

The use of a song in complete opposition to its context in the play is most apparent in Juno and Mary's singing of 'Home to our Mountains', an area from Verdi's *Il Trovatore*. In the opera, the song is sung by the Troubadour to his mother, who has just been disturbed by frightful visions. In the play, the situation is in reverse; it is the son, Johnny, who has just seen frightful visions of Tancred's body. Johnny is never a source of comfort to his mother. The words of the song, too, are in direct contrast to the troubled state of their home: 'Home to our mountains,/Let us return love,/There in thy young days/Peace had its reign'. A less poignant irony is commented on within the play: Captain Boyle sings 'Sweet Spirit, hear my prayer', another opulent aria from the opera *Lurline*, about the Lorelei myth, meant to be sung by a water-nymph, therefore especially comic in the seafaring 'Captain's' 'self-honouring voice'. As Juno tartly comments, 'it's not for a job he's prayin'!' Captain Boyle's 'I will be true to you' comes into the same category of insincere pledges, as he is untrue before the beginning of the next act. The irony of such snatches of song can be conscious: Joxer's 'the anchor's weigh'd, farewell, remember me', from the opera *The Americans*, is about a heartbreaking parting of lovers, 'Doubt not a constant heart like mine', which he is using sarcastically to bid yet another farewell to the friend he has betrayed. He uses a similar sarcasm in greeting Maisie Madigan on her unwelcome mission of taking back her goods, with Thomas Davis's 'The Welcome'—'Come in the evening or come in the morning', which goes on 'Kisses and welcome you'll find here before you', in direct contradiction of the situation.

O'Casey's most profoundly ironic use of song in the play is, however to comment on jingoism. Even the name 'Tancred' points to this purpose: Rossini's opera *Tancred* (1813) in which the knight Tancred tries to free the small nation of Syracuse from its oppressors, had been taken up as a byword of passionate nationalism, a heroic vision of modern national idealism.* (Here, ironically, he is killed by a comrade professing the same ideals.) The Irish songs sung in the play are bitterly unheroic in their contexts. The patriotic 'I met with Napper Tandy and he took me by the hand' is used mockingly by Joxer about the priest hypocritically shaking Boyle's hand. The cheapest expression of Irish nationalism in the play is blared out by the gramophone. 'If you're Irish, come into the parlour' is blarneying, paddy-Irish camaraderie of the most destructive sort: 'If your name is Timothy or Pat,/So long as you come from Ireland, there's a welcome on the mat ... Whoever you are, you're one of us/If you're Irish, this is the place for you'. It is at this point that Needle Nugent comes into the Boyles' parlour with his plea for respect for the Irish people's 'National regard for the dead'; these are the two sides of empty Irish jargon.

Otherwise, the patriotic sentiments expressed are *not* from Irish sources: Joxer's 'Yes: let me like a soldier fall/Upon some open plain/This breast expanding for the ball/To blot out ev'ry stain' is from *Maritana*, an English opera; his 'Breathes there the man, with soul so dead,/Who never to himself hath said,/This is my own, my native land' is a parlour ballad based on Walter Scott's 'Lay of the last Minstrel' and is about Scotland. 'Pack up your troubles in your old kit bag' is the most searing example of this; not only does it reflect on Boyle's and Joxer's irresponsible levity with its inane refrain 'smile, smile, smile'; it was a British marching song of the 1914–1918 War, and was sung by the hated Black and Tans when they were the occupying troops in Ireland. What is more, its subject is a soldier, Private Perks, who

*Benjamin Disraeli's *Tancred: or the new Crusade* (1847) used Tancred's story as a solution for England's political doubt and despair.

recruited soldiers for the British Army; the recruiting of Irishmen to fight for Britain was one of the most controversial issues in the Free State Treaty. O'Casey hated jingoism on the Irish side; such use of English jingo underlines the stupidity and futility of any jingo; that such a song could be sung underlines how little reality the idea of nationalism or republicanism had for the average Dublin man.

## Tragi-comedy

The tragedies played out in *Juno and the Paycock* are the destructiveness and the waste of the Boyles' marriage; the tragedy of Johnny, also wasted and destroyed; the particular tragedy of Juno's loss of her son and the ancillary tragedy of Mrs Tancred representing all mothers; the tragedy of being poor. And over all, the tragedy of Ireland destroyed and wasted by civil war; Irish men, having fought together against her occupiers in two bloody combats, now fighting one another. On these tragedies is laid the comedy—the quick backchat, the boasts and stories, the farce. All the comic parts, although funny in themselves, make their effect by being overlaid upon these tragic themes. The mood of the play oscillates: the party scene, for example, moves from religious discussion to Johnny's terror, to comic songs, to a funeral, to more comic songs, to the Mobilizer coming for Johnny. The end of the play moves from Juno's optimistic 'we'll work together for the sake of the baby' to her recessional mourning for Johnny as they leave, then reverts to comedy with Captain Boyle and Joxer—though their comedy in itself is tragic because of their obliviousness of the truth.

Straightforwardly farcical situations occur—Juno hiding to catch Joxer and Captain Boyle as they make themselves at home; Joxer hiding on the roof and jumping in when he hears Captain Boyle say he is 'done with Joxer'. The public performance of certain private functions has its farcical side, like Captain Boyle getting into his moleskin trousers and looking for his braces, or Jerry incongruously trying to kiss Mary's 'little, small, white hand' in front of an indignant Captain Boyle.

But on the whole the farce is verbal—the repartee, the comic catchphrases, the cumulative comedy of repetition. There is the comedy of dialect and mispronunciation; of pompous phrases misused, of ludicrous images. Inflation and deflation can both be comic: Captain Boyle's inflation of his fantasies with invention, exaggeration, rhetoric and bombast, Juno's facility in knocking him down.

The ignorance that prompts Joxer's and Captain Boyle's mistakes makes us laugh at first but is fundamentally tragic; their idleness, drunkenness and deviousness give numerous opportunities for comedy but are in themselves wasteful and destructive. Tenement life gives rise to farcical situations but is in reality grim. Thus the superficialities of certain circumstances of Dublin life make an audience laugh, whereas they are tragic if examined in full. The means of saving the Irish from their circumstances fail in this place; heroes become cowards, nationalism becomes jingoism, Labour humanitarianism becomes inhumanity. These are the tragedies of the play; the only optimistic note is Juno's step away from a tragic life to a positive future. We see not the destruction of her character but the ennobling of it; but this is accomplished only through tragedy.

# Part 4

# Hints for study

## Points for detailed study

*Juno and the Paycock* is an energetic play, in which O'Casey makes his points clearly and economically. Although it belongs to the mixed or 'impure' genre of tragi-comedy, it is formal, almost symmetrical in its structure and characterisation. You will find it useful to consider the play under the following aspects: the four linked plots; themes; conflicts; characterisation; the Irish context; O'Casey's methods.

### The four linked plots

The formality of the play's construction invites individual analysis of its four plots, each of which has its own 'story', its own stage in each act, and its own climax (*a-e*). Each plot, however, affects the others in some way, and the points of intersection are worth studying (*f*). The characters common to the plots change their relationships sharply in each act, with a different one appearing central to the whole play (*g*).

(*a*) Johnny's plot in Act I is one of mounting tension. Notice the examples of his growing nervousness and how successive interruptions add to the tension.

In Act II Johnny's story reaches a psychological climax in the revelation of his guilt through his vision of the dead Tancred, and a material climax when the Mobilizer connects him with the army and with Tancred's death. See how O'Casey uses Johnny's religion in Act I to show his desire for protection, in Act II to reveal his guilt.

In Act III this plot reaches its inevitable conclusion when Johnny is taken away to be executed for betraying his comrade. Notice how he turns furiously on each member of his family as the pressure on him grows.

(*b*) Mary's plot shows her with Jerry in Act I, though their love affair has ended; study particularly her personal independence and her active trade unionist principles.

In Act II she is engaged to marry Bentham; note that we only know this by hearsay; they have no love-scene.

In Act III Mary is rejected for her pregnancy by all except her mother. Jerry's rejection of her after his protestations of love is the climax of Mary's plot. There are similarities between all the men's scornful reactions; see also the symmetrical contrasts between Jerry and Bentham.

(c) The plot of the will is introduced at the end of Act I; watch the reactions of each character to its announcement.

In Act II the Boyles' anticipation of the money displays their spendthrift vulgarity; notice how being 'rich' affects each character.

In Act III the will is declared invalid, leaving the Boyles worse off than before. See how they react to this: it did promise them all escape.

(d) In the story of Juno and Captain Boyle, Act I establishes them as hostile antagonists, he an idler, she a worker. Notice how they use their tongues as weapons against each other, and that Joxer is Juno's 'rival' for Captain Boyle's loyalties.

In Act II they are much less antagonistic; note their similar tastes in spending.

In Act III Captain Boyle fails Juno in every crisis, forcing her to the realisation that she must free herself from him. Note the points at which he fails his family: when the furniture is taken away, when Mary is pregnant, when Johnny is killed.

(e) The climaxes in these plots are of different kinds. Johnny's reaches its peak in the revelation of his guilt, of which his arrest is the inevitable consequence. The will's invalidity, after its supposed realisation, is materially an anti-climax, but dramatically a climax. In the Juno-Captain Boyle plot, the moment of climax is that in which she realises that he is worthless and hopeless and that she must leave him if she and the next generation are to go forward. This is also the climax of the whole play. The coda or tail-piece in which Captain Boyle comes back drunk is potent anti-climax; it shows the man Juno has left, why she has left him, and the tragic extent of his blindness.

(f) Notice the points at which these plots intersect. Captain Boyle's callous attitude to Mary's pregnancy provokes Juno's threat to leave. Johnny's death precipitates her realisation that her husband is useless and that she must leave him. The will eases their relationship; its failure bars any escape for Johnny or for Mary. Bentham is the instrument of the will, of its failure, and of Mary's downfall.

(g) Each act has one central figure to whom the others relate. In Act I it is Juno; ties radiate outwards from her, with Mary in a practical mother-daughter bond, with Johnny in a more complex relationship;

Juno is proud yet disappointed, protective and conscious of his wounds. Strong antagonism links her with Captain Boyle, fear and hatred with Joxer. She is deferential to Bentham, familiar with Jerry. Outside these ties with Juno are the uneasy friendships of Mary and Jerry and of Captain Boyle and Joxer.

In Act II Johnny is the focal figure, to whom Juno is protective, Mary concerned, Captain Boyle irritable and irritating. His hysterical vision is provoked by Bentham; he is linked to his battalion by the Mobilizer. Around these are other relationships: Mary's with Bentham, Captain Boyle's with Joxer.

In Act III, Mary is at the centre, rejected by all in turn except Juno, with whom she is closely allied, Juno's links with her husband and son being broken by the failure of one and the death of the other. All the other characters prey upon the Boyle family from outside.

## Themes

The major recurrent themes in the play, often differently viewed by different characters, are: (a) nationalism; (b) religion; (c) poverty; (d) the Labour movement.

(a) Nationalism. This means heroism and principles to Johnny, danger, waste and loss of lives and limbs to Juno—although she is proud of Johnny's exploits. It is also seen as an opportunity for profit (Nugent, Captain Boyle) or for grim retribution (the Irregulars). Notice also how easily nationalism becomes jingoism, in the mouths of Needle Nugent or Mrs Tancred's neighbours, or in Captain Boyle's last boasts.

(b) Religion also means different things to each character; to Johnny an unavailing protection against his guilt, to Mary an empty promise. To Juno it originally means ritual and help, though she is finally forced to the humanist query 'what can God do agen the stupidity o' men?' Jerry is 'all man an' no God'; Bentham proposes theosophy as the fount of all wisdom. Religion is no true spiritual comfort to anyone in the play, and no prayers are granted; it is often mentioned in its social, political and historical aspects.

(c) Poverty is presented as depriving not only of material things but also dignity, joy and integrity. It fosters the characters' worst faults—anger, ignorance, idleness, drunkenness, vulgarity. Poverty traps; it is difficult to rise above it materially or intellectually. Notice how all the characters wish to escape their poor environment, and see how well O'Casey paints the claustrophobic atmosphere of the tenement.

(*d*) The Labour movement. O'Casey sets forth the highest Labour ideals and makes his characters fail to live up to them. Jerry is earnest, dedicated and authoritative but lacks the one vital quality, humanity. Mary loses her emancipated principles in the female dilemma. Notice the obstacles in the way of Labour: the stubborn idleness of Boyle and Joxer, Juno's disbelief in Labour solidarity, Johnny's inability to work.

## Conflicts

Our attention is drawn to several clearly-defined conflicts by speech, action and stage directions.

(*a*) education *versus* environment

(*b*) Labour principles *versus* practice

(*c*) nationalism *versus* humanitarianism

(*d*) romanticism *versus* reality

(*a*) The conflict between education and environment is seen most clearly in Mary, torn between two forces, her environment dragging her back, her reading pushing her forward. The other characters display ignorance in various forms from imprudence (Juno, Captain Boyle) to stupidity (Captain Boyle, Joxer).

(*b*) The conflict between Labour principles and practice is personified by Jerry, full of words but failing in deeds. He has some knowledge but not enough to broaden his power for the benefit of all. Mary has the idealistic Labour vision, without the opportunity to impose it; Juno, who disapproves of the elementary principles of trade unionism, is the one character to practise true humanitarianism.

(*c*) The conflict between nationalist principles professing concern for the people of Ireland, and nationalist practice resulting in their destruction dominates the play. Johnny's heroics are counteracted by his cowardice and treachery. Abstract nationalism is contrasted with personal loss by Mrs Tancred and Juno.

(*d*) The conflict between romanticism and reality appears in several guises; Mary's romantic love for Bentham is at odds with his real nature; Juno's romantic idea that Captain Boyle can be the head of the family clashes with the truth. Captain Boyle's own storytelling is the extremity of romantic fantasy divorced from real life. Romantic nationalism and a romantic faith in the externals of religion also conflict with reality.

## Characterisation

O'Casey's skilful characterisation is evident in these people, apparently very real, yet heightened almost to the point of caricature, like Captain Boyle and Joxer who must be funny yet convey a tragic message. The characters fall into two categories: those who are static (a) and those who develop in the course of the play (b).

(a) Static characters: Captain Boyle, Joxer and Johnny are static. We may learn more about them, but they do not change direction; this is one of the tragic points about Captain Boyle. Nothing can develop him; he is as irresponsible at the end of the play as at the beginning. Joxer is the same devious sponger throughout. We know that Johnny is a coward before our suspicions of his guilt are confirmed. Maisie Madigan, Needle Nugent and Mrs Tancred are also static characters.

(b) Developing characters, who change for better or worse because of events in the play, are Mary, Jerry and Juno. Mary loses much of her independent spirit, but she grows more protective to her mother, and she achieves dignity and clarity of vision in the face of Jerry's humiliating rejection. Jerry develops for the worse; his professed humanity might have survived many things but cannot withstand the news of Mary's pregnancy. Juno is the one character who is strengthened and ennobled by what she goes through.

## The Irish context

O'Casey chose Dublin characters and a Dublin setting because he was familiar with them, because the language was theatrically original, and because events at the time of which he wrote were intrinsically dramatic. Although he was concerned for the mass of the Irish nation, particularly the coming generation, he was not concerned only with Ireland. He chooses these familiar poor as representatives of the world's poor.

The Irish context serves the following functions: (a) to give reality of setting; (b) to give authenticity to the speech; (c) to reinforce the characterisation; (d) to use dramatically issues raised by recent history.

(a) The reality of setting is apparent in O'Casey's stage directions, in local references, in Dublin street salesman, contemporary patent medicines. The peculiar density of the Irish tenement world also emphasises the claustrophobia of poverty.

(b) The accuracy of the speech lends conviction to the whole play. Even when dramatically heightened, the language appears natural.

(c) The characterisation of the play is reinforced by the recognisable Dublin types portrayed—the out-of-work, the pub-goer, the big talker, the dominant Irish matriarch.

(d) Recent Irish history raised a number of moral and practical issues like those of Civil War, the beginnings of a Labour movement, the birth struggles of a small nation and their effect on the next generation.

## Methods

The most frequently used technical devices are: (a) irony; (b) contrast; (c) repetition; (d) 'realism'; (e) symbolism; (f) literary references; (g) musical references; (h) stage directions.

(a) Irony includes the overall irony of life in which nationalism leads to civil war, or individual ironies like the betrayal of Johnny's guilt by the votive light that he relies on for protection. Sometimes the audience knows something the characters do not, as when Captain Boyle is too drunk to see that his family has gone; sometimes the other characters know something the speaker does not, as when Juno plans to take Mary away with the non-existent money. There is much verbal irony in the form of sarcasm, and irony of allusion where a song or poem quoted conflicts with the situation in the play.

(b) Many major points are made by contrast—as that between principles professed and actions taken. Sharp contrasts are drawn between characters like Jerry and Bentham. Contrasts between party and funeral change the mood of the play; the contrast between Juno's grief and Boyle's drunken return underlines the tragedy of the play.

(c) Repetition can be of scenes, like Jerry's love-scene with Mary; or of phrases for comic or for tragic effect. Johnny's final repetition of the Hail Mary, last heard at Tancred's funeral, links their deaths; Juno's repetition of Mrs Tancred's elegy and prayer emphasises their relevance to the play.

(d) Realism of speech, settings, furniture, 'business', Dublin types, make the 'material' side of the play convincing, which paradoxically reinforces its symbolic side.

(e) The symbolism of the play lies in simple things like the protecting votive light extinguished just before Johnny's arrest. The Virgin Mary symbolises sorrowing motherhood; Mary's baby represents future generations. The gramophone stands for cheap luxury, and money symbolises escape.

(*f*) Literary references are used by O'Casey to reinforce his theme, and for irony. Notice in particular the Ibsen references which form a commentary on the theme of liberation.

(*g*) Musical references are used partly for comedy—opportunities for Joxer to forget his songs. They also represent a fantasy world unlike the true one. The words of the ballads sung or mentioned often make an ironic commentary on the situation in the play.

(*h*) O'Casey used stage directions not only to give details of his characters' appearance and mannerisms, but to reveal their inner conflicts. Note Mary's 'two forces', Juno's possibilities compared with her present drudgery, Jerry's insufficient breadth of knowledge. Captain Boyle has a self-honouring voice, Joxer a twitching movement meant to be ingratiating, Bentham a very high opinion of himself.

# Selection of material

There are many memorable phrases in *Juno and the Paycock* which convey briefly and unmistakably the colouring of a character or scene. You will have observed that such phrases are very often repeated in different places and in different tones. Certain key speeches are repeated in full, like Mrs Tancred's elegy and prayer echoed by Juno. You will find both types of repetition helpful in writing about the play. Look too for quotations that will crystallise dramatic peaks and turning points in the play, which mark a change in mood or pace. For characterisation, look for phrases that emphasise habitual traits or verbal mannerisms, and for points at which the characters' reactions to news reveal their characters. Note examples of repetition, and key speeches that embody the message of the play.

## Dramatic peaks

There are certain moments in the play which have been led up to with mounting tension: Johnny's cry of fear 'Mother o' God, the light's afther goin' out' has been prepared for by many references to the protection of the votive light. The news from Mrs Madigan, completed by Juno, comes after Juno's agonised wait—'Some poor fella's been found, an' they think it's, it's . . .' 'Johnny, Johnny'. After the increasing tension of knocks at the door and mysterious visitors through two acts, the moment at which the Mobilizer appears and says simply 'Quarther-Masther Boyle' is one of great drama; so is the moment when the Irregular confirms Johnny's betrayal, after all the hints and growing certainty through the play: 'Poor Tancred was an oul' comrade o' yours, but you didn't think o' that when you gave him away to the gang that sent him to his grave'.

## Turning points

There are several definite turning points after which the given facts of the play have to be revised. Notice particularly Johnny's scream and his explanation 'I seen him ... I seen Robbie Tancred kneelin' down before the statue ... an' I seen the woun's bleedin' in his breast'. Followed by his defensive 'Oh, why did he look at me like that? ... it wasn't my fault that he was done in', this is our moral confirmation that he has betrayed Tancred, and it changes the entire nature of the play from comedy to tragedy. Another such turning point is the announcement that Mary is pregnant: 'Mary's goin' to have a baby in a short time'. Jerry's 'My God, Mary, have you fallen as low as that?' is a distinct turning point in our estimation of his character: up to now he has seemed worthy, earnest, humanitarian. Juno's great moment of realisation and decision marks another 'watershed': 'Let your father furrage for himself now; I've done all I could an' it was all no use—he'll be hopeless to the end of his days.'.

## Change of mood or pace

You will find numerous examples of change of pace and mood in the play: the switch from Jerry's love-talk, 'Let me kiss your hand, your little, tiny, white hand', to farce with Captain Boyle's 'Chiselurs don't care a damn now about their parents, they're bringin' their fathers' grey hairs down with sorra to the grave, an' laughin' at it, laughin' at it'. The entrance of Mrs Tancred in mid-party is another such change: 'Whether they're up or down — it won't bring me darlin' boy from the grave'. The swing back to the party is heralded by Maisie Madigan's banal 'What about Mr Boyle's song before we start th' gramophone?' and there is another swing back with the arrival of Needle Nugent:' 'Are you going' to have that thing bawlin' an' the funeral of Mrs Tancred's son passin' the house?'

## Characterisation

Choose phrases that illustrate the characters' individuality and others that show them as representatives of a category—their mouthing of 'principles'. The stage directions give insights into each character. So do their remarks about each other: Jerry is 'a good boy, sober, able to talk'; Bentham a 'Micky Dazzler', Boyle a 'paycock', Johnny 'very sensitive, all of a sudden'. The characters' own words reveal them, even such simple words as Mary's dignified 'yes, Jerry, I have fallen as low as that' or Juno's 'whinin' an' whingin' isn't goin' to do any good'. Points at which characters become 'mouthpieces' include Johnny's 'I'd do it agen, ma, I'd do it agen; for a principle's a principle', Mary's 'What's the use of belongin' to a trades union if you won't stand up for your principles' and Jerry's 'With Labour, Mary, Humanity is above everything; we are the Leaders in the fight for a new life', ironically placed just before his rejection of her.

## Reactions

You will notice that O'Casey uses the announcement of certain pieces of news to reveal character through the various reactions to it. Upon the announcement of the will, Mary sees simply the money: 'A fortune, father, a fortune'; Johnny sees escape: 'We'll be able to get out o' this place now an' go somewhere we're not known'; Mrs Boyle shows her latent sympathy with her husband: 'You won't have to trouble about a job for awhile, Jack'. Reactions to the news that the will is invalid are equally revealing: Joxer's the usual cliché, 'him that goes a borrowin' goes a sorrowin''; Mrs Boyle's, after three 'I don't believe it's', is 'Now I know why Bentham left poor Mary in th' lurch; I can see it all now—oh, is there not even a middlin' honest man left in th' world?'. Johnny's is vicious—I'll tell you what I think of you, father an' all as you are'. The news of Mary's pregnancy shows Captain Boyle first as comically uncomprehending: 'Goin' to have a baby!—my God, what'll Bentham say when he hears that?' then as selfish: 'A pretty show I'll be to Joxer an' to that oul' wan, Madigan! Amn't I afther goin' through enough without havin' to go through this!' Johnny's reaction is heartless: 'She should be dhriven out o' th' house she's brought disgrace on!' Notice also reactions to Mrs Tancred, to the funeral, and to the news of Johnny's death.

## Repetition

Some of the repetition is of the characters' 'slogans' like Joxer's use of 'darlin' or 'daarlin', or Captain Boyle's 'I've a little spirit left in me still'. Note the repetitions in which the tone changes—'the whole worl's in a state o' chassis' is used first farcically about Jerry kissing Mary's hand, then as part of Captain Boyle's 'business' conversation, and finally in the last line of the play as a tragic intimation of his blind generalisation. 'What is the stars, what is the stars?' is echoed first sychophantically, later treacherously by Joxer. The repetition of Jerry's love scene with Mary emphasises the irony of his 'No matter what happens, you'll always be the same to me'. The Hail Mary sung at Tancred's funeral and recited at Johnny's arrest connects the two dramatically and symbolically, while Juno's repetition of Mrs Tancred's words about her son is in itself a statement about the brotherhood of man.

## Key speeches

The three sections of Mrs Tancred's elegy and prayer for her son also convey three aspects of the play's message lyrically and poignantly. 'What's the pains I suffered bringin' him into the world to carry him to his cradle, to the pains I'm sufferin' now, carryin' him out o' the world to bring him to his grave!' is the expression of bereaved motherhood. The formality of her words about Mrs Manning, 'An' now here's the two of us oul' women, standin' one on each side of a scales o' sorra, balanced be the bodies of our two dead darlin' sons' is not echoed by Juno, but she steps into the balance on the other side herself. 'Blessed Virgin, where were you when me darlin' son was riddled with bullets? . . . Sacred Heart of the Crucified Jesus, take away our hearts o' stone . . . an' give us hearts o' flesh! . . . Take away this murdherin' hate . . . an' give us Thine own eternal love' is a highly charged poetic expression of the play's message. But that comes through too in more plebeian phrases: Juno's 'Ah, what can God do agen the stupidity o' men?' or another Joxer quotation: 'Man's inhumanity to man makes countless thousands mourn'. Mrs Tancred's 'scales o' sorra' is just as well expressed in Juno's 'Ah, why didn't I remember that then he wasn't a Diehard or a Stater, but only a poor dead son!'. Juno's forward impetus toward the next generation is simply expressed in 'we'll work together for the sake of the baby'. Captain Boyle's 'What did th' likes of her, born in a tenement house, want with readin'' reveals the depths of ignorance born of poverty, another of the play's themes. Juno's crisp answers very often encapsulate the play's messages. She counters Mary's conventional 'My poor little child that'll have no father' with the remark of one of a sisterhood of strong women: 'It'll have what's far better—it'll have two mothers'. To Needle Nugent's 'Have none of yous any respect for the Irish people's National regard for the dead? she sums up the play's anti-jingoistic message: 'Maybe, Needle Nugent, it's nearly time we have a little less respect for the dead, an' a little more regard for the livin''. And to Boyle's indifferent 'We've nothin' to do with these things, one way or t'other. That's the Government's business, an' let them do what we're payin' them for doin'', her 'I'd like to know how a body's not to mind these things ... Sure, if it's not our business, I don't know whose business it is', states the play's message that it is each man's duty to be concerned for himself and for humanity.

# Arrangement of material

The headings in the previous section above will help in arranging your material; consider also the following groupings: language; characterisation; context; and message.

## Language

O'Casey uses Dublin speech, fragments of verse and song, rhetoric and Biblical language blended together to form a natural-sounding yet dramatic language. Notice here points like irony (a character saying one thing and practising another); notice, too, points at which the speech changes the mood of the play to lyrical, comic, tragic.

## Characterisation

The main characters clearly voice their outlook and beliefs—Mary's, Johnny's and Jerry's jargon, Johnny's superstitious faith, Juno's steadfastness, Captain Boyle's rhetoric and fantasy, Joxer's sycophancy. Arrange your material to show also the different aspects of the developing characters—Mary in independence and dependence, Juno in her nagging, in her trivial spending and in her noble final phase. You will also wish to make the links between characters who mirror or contrast with each other, as Bentham and Jerry, or Juno, Maisie Madigan and Mrs Tancred.

## Context

The Irish context of the play is apparent in the current civil war, the recent East Rising, and past events like the famine and the Fenian rebellion. Remember too that the play had a contemporary time-context—it was written only four years after the events in it were supposed to have taken place.

## Message

The message of the play can be considered under several headings—the themes of poverty, labour, duty to one's family, the harmfulness of jingoism and of false heroics. You will find it convenient to consider all these separately while bearing in mind that the total message is that mishandling any of them obstructs the liberty of the individual and the progress of mankind.

## Questions

(a) O'Casey wrote: 'Even in the most commonplace of realistic plays the symbol can never be absent'. Discuss realism and symbolism in *Juno and the Paycock*.

(b) Write on dramatic tension and anti-climax in *Juno and the Paycock*.

(c) Discuss O'Casey's use of dialect in *Juno and the Paycock*.

(d) Can you distinguish between the tragedy, comedy and melodrama in *Juno and the Paycock*?

(e) Write about O'Casey's use of parallels in *Juno and the Paycock*.

(f) Consider the idea of commitment in *Juno and the Paycock*.

(g) Has *Juno and the Paycock* one message or many?

(h) Can *Juno and the Paycock* be interpreted as a feminist play?

(i) 'No real character can be put in a play unless some of the reality is taken out of him through the heightening, widening, and deepening of the character by the dramatist who created him'. Discuss this statement of O'Casey's with reference to *Juno and the Paycock*.

(j) 'There is only one complete character in *Juno and the Paycock* —Juno herself. Upon her hangs the weight of the play'. Comment.

(k) 'The turbulent history through which Ireland had been living breaks into these tenements. As a direct action it is on the streets, and the people crowded in the houses react to it, in essential ways, as if it were an action beyond and outside them' (Raymond Williams). Does your reading of *Juno and the Paycock* prompt you to agree?

(l) How far is *Juno and the Paycock* a specifically Irish play?

## Some suggested answers

### (b) Dramatic tension and anti-climax in *Juno and the Paycock*

O'Casey builds up dramatic tension in the play at different levels—from Captain Boyle's high-rising rhetoric to the grim outer tension of the civil war going on outside. And he consistently knocks it down again in anti-climax. The immediate effect of this anti-climax may be comic or tragic, depending on the situation, but in the long view it will always be ironic.

In purely verbal tension and anti-climax, you might use Captain Boyle's seafaring tale of 'sailin' from the Gulf o' Mexico to the Antanartic Ocean' as a comic example and Johnny's declarations of love to Mary as a tragic one. Captain Boyle builds up with hints of dreadful things he has seen, dreadful experiences he has had, and blow upon blow of wind until he asks himself his great question, echoed by Joxer and followed by another, the final question bringing the whole edifice tumbling down—'what is the moon?', not really a climactic question at all. Jerry's renewed protestations of love for Mary are built up with equal pressure—we remember that he is a skilled public speaker. His crescendo of rhetorical passion grows from his love for Mary, 'greater and deeper than ever', encompasses Labour and Humanity to a repeated 'I love you, I love you'—and is let down in anticlimax at the crucial moment with fear in his eyes and 'have you fallen as low as that?'. In both of these cases O'Casey inflates his audience's expectation and suddenly deflates it, in an ironic revelation of the speaker's character.

Tension is built up in the action of the play by the series of interrupters and callers—the sewing machine salesman, the 'fella in a trench coat', the coal vendor, all against the background of Johnny's nervousness. The quiet Mobilizer is an anti-climax after all the preceding 'tathera-raa's. There is a similar anti-climax when the Irregulars come to take Johnny to his death—after the ever-increasing tension throughout the play, the visions, the nerves, the alarms, Johnny is taken away with a few terse words from some men who have 'no time to waste'—taken away as ignominiously as the furniture.

As Juno waits with Mary an hour later, there are two sources of tension centred on her—Johnny's death and Mary's pregnancy. This is not 'suspense''—we know Johnny's fate and Mary's condition: it is the dramatic tension of awaiting Juno's reaction. We have one moment to appreciate the truly climactic step she is taking as she leaves home and husband and goes forward to build a new life for Mary's child—a step that all the play's action has been leading up to, and which is its highest dramatic point. Then the anti-climax strikes—or shuffles in—with Captain Boyle and Joxer. Boyle has actually seen Juno and Mary leaving with the police, but 'the blinds is down' (the sign of a death in a house), and he cannot really see. He is 'blind drunk'. The effect of this anti-climax is to stress that he will be 'hopeless to the end of his days'; coming after Juno's optimistic step forward it is also an ironic and profoundly pessimistic statement about mankind's capacity for understanding.

## (f) The idea of commitment in *Juno and the Paycock*

O'Casey was committed throughout his life to the liberation of the individual, the race and the class. He was a political worker, joining and revitalising nationalist and labour organisations in his youth and professing Communism in later life. His early experience of poverty had made him see how difficult it was to overcome alone; he believed that only in working together could men liberate and educate themselves.

In *Juno and the Paycock*, commitment and detachment are examined in the domestic and the political sense. Captain Boyle fails his family because of his detachment from them; he is not concerned for them; he is incapable of giving them either moral or material support. He fails his country in the same way; he is too detached to care about the civil war: 'we've nothin' to do with these things'.

Yet the play makes plain that over-commitment is just as dangerous: the senseless dedication to 'principles' is splitting the country in two. Johnny's 'Ireland only half free can never be at peace while she has a son left to pull a trigger' shows a commitment to uncompromising nationalism that can only harm the nation.

In the domestic sense Juno expresses the idea of commitment, of the dedication of the group to the good of its members. She and Mary will 'work together for the sake of the baby'. In the political sense she sees that 'regard for the living' must outweigh 'the Irish people's National regard for the dead' that Needle Nugent promotes.

Outside the Boyle family, Joxer, Needle Nugent and Maisie Madigan—a sponger, a profiteer, and a superficially sentimental, generous woman who is in reality self-seeking—are examples of non-commitment. And even Jerry, who is supposedly committed to Labour ideas, fails to live up to them. At first sight a sensible and worthy worker for humanity's good, he cannot rise as Juno can to the smaller commitment, to 'love thy neighbour' as well as to fight for one's party. In them all, O'Casey condemns a society without that spirit which Joxer cannot grasp, of 'all for one and one for all'; the spirit of communal effort.

## (g) Has *Juno and the Paycock* one message or many?

Several morals can be drawn from the play: that war, especially civil war, is futile; that poverty is degrading; that 'man's inhumanity to man makes countless thousands mourn'. A case could be made for including the idea of individual responsibility as one of the play's messages—the indifference of Captain Boyle in matters of politics matches his detachment from his family. But the overall moral of the play could be seen as a combination of these three factors: that only in working together and doing their simple duty by their families can men improve the human condition. To do this they must avoid excesses like false heroics and false jingoistic nationalism, and they must free themselves from the bonds of convention in order to realise themselves. Poverty is the common enemy that prevents man from carrying out this simple duty.

---

### (h) Can *Juno and the Paycock* be interpreted as a feminist play?

---

O'Casey had a great admiration for his mother: many of his heroines are based on her and have that strength in the face of adversity which he admired in her. It is this quality rather than any 'feminist' message that he seeks to show as an example: he advocates it as a quality that humanity must develop if it is to go forward.

Like Ibsen and Shaw, whose plays have often been misinterpreted as extreme examples of feminism, O'Casey used the current situation of women as an oppressed 'class' to express his disapproval of any group being subordinate to any other. Like their heroines, Mary and Juno are fettered and dragged down by their circumstances, some caused by the men who surround them. Traditionally, woman is fettered by man. Juno sees that Mary can only grow and live if she leaves this home. Juno herself is deadened by her life, her home and her marriage. Her liberation depends on her leaving—but it is the liberation of the individual, not of the woman, that matters.

Juno's statement that the baby 'will have what's far betther—it'll have two mothers' shows a faith in feminine independence, industry and sense. O'Casey saw women as being realistic in their approach to life in general and to war in particular. It is women who suffer the worst pain of war—they have to see their houses raided and their sons killed for 'a principle'. Time and again in *Juno and the Paycock* it is Juno who sees that bullets and bombs bring not glory but 'the finishin' touch—'You lost your best principle, me boy, when you lost your arm'. Women know that they are the victims, the sisterhood on each side of the scales of sorrow, while the men play soldiers like Captain Boyle—'Commandant Kelly died . . . in them arms . . . tell me Volunteer Butties . . . says he . . . that I died for Ireland'. It is this feminine wisdom that makes Juno see respect for the living as more important than respect for the dead and that the civil war is women's business which cannot be ignored as Captain Boyle wishes. Again this is a wisdom that O'Casey admires in women and advocates for all. The right he claims for women is to follow their instinctive feminine good sense, and to lead others less wise.

# Part 5

# Suggestions for further reading

## The text

The text used in compiling these notes was: Sean O'Casey, *Three Plays (Juno and the Paycock, The Shadow of a Gunman, The Plough and the Stars)*, Macmillan, St Martin's Press, London, 1957, reprinted 1975.

## Other works by Sean O'Casey

*Plays*

*Collected Plays*, 4 volumes, Macmillan, London and New York, 1949–51.

*Five One-Act Plays*, Macmillan, St Martin's Press, London, 1958.

*Three More Plays (The Silver Tassie, Purple Dust, Red Roses for Me)*, with an introduction by J. C. Trewin, Macmillan, London, 1965; St Martin's Press, New York, 1965.

*Autobiographies:*

*I Knock at the Door: swift glances back at things that made me* (covers the years 1880–1890), Macmillan, London and New York, 1939.

*Pictures in the Hallway* (covers 1891–1904), Macmillan, London and New York, 1942.

*Drums under the Window* (covers 1905–1916), Macmillan, London and New York, 1945.

*Inishfallen Fare Thee Well* (covers 1916–26, including the years that *Juno and the Paycock* was written and staged), Macmillan, London and New York, 1949.

*Rose and Crown* (covers 1926–1934), Macmillan, London and New York, 1952.

*Sunset and Evening Star* (covers 1934–1953), Macmillan, London and New York, 1954.

These give an excellent, heightened picture of O'Casey's life and times; they were also published as *Mirror in my House, the Autobiographies of Sean O'Casey*, 2 volumes, Macmillan, New York, 1956, reprinted as *Autobiographies*, 2 volumes, Macmillan, London, 1963.

*Criticism, articles and stories*

*Blasts and Benedictions*, Articles and stories selected and introduced by Ronald Ayling, Macmillan, London and St Martin's Press, New York, 1967. This contains articles, stories and occasional writings on the theatre, Ireland and people.

*Feathers from the Green Crow, Sean O'Casey, 1905-1925*, edited by Robert Hogan, London, Macmillan, 1963. This is a good collection of O'Casey's early work, including ballads, plays, articles and stories.

*The Flying Wasp: A laughing look-over of what has been said about the things of the theatre by the English dramatic critics*, Macmillan, London and New York, 1937. This gives a good idea of O'Casey's views about his own and others' dramatic work.

*Under a Colored Cap: Articles merry and mournful with comments and a song*, Macmillan, London, 1963; St Martin's Press, New York, 1963. Articles, essays and personal reminiscences.

*Windfalls*, Macmillan, London and New York, 1934. This contains early poems, short stories and plays.

*The Letters of Sean O'Casey*, Vol. I. 1910–1941, edited by David Krause, Cassell, London, 1975.

---

## General reading

AYLING, RONALD (ED.) *Sean O'Casey*; Modern Judgments Series, Macmillan, London, 1969. A collection of essays on O'Casey's life and work.

BENSTOCK, BERNARD: *Paycocks and Others. Sean O'Casey's World*, Gill and Macmillan, Dublin, 1977; Barnes and Noble Books, New York, 1977. Good on O'Casey's characters.

COWASJEE, SAROS: *O'Casey*, Writers and Critics, Oliver and Boyd, Edinburgh and London, 1966. The best brief assessment of O'Casey's work and opinions.

GOLDSTONE, HERBERT: *In Search of Community: the Achievement of Sean O'Casey*, Mercier Press, Cork and Dublin, 1972. A good examination of O'Casey's views on social commitment.

HOGAN, ROBERT: *The Experiments of Sean O'Casey*, St Martin's Press, New York, 1960. An excellent assessment of O'Casey's dramatic techniques.

KRAUSE, DAVID: *Sean O'Casey, the man and his work*, Macgibbon and Kee, London, 1960. The best study of O'Casey's work related to his biography.

MALONE, MAUREEN: *The Plays of Sean O'Casey*, Crosscurrents/ Modern Critiques, Southern Illinois University Press, Carbondale and Edwardsville, 1969. This sets the plays in the context of current events.

## Bibliography

MIKHAIL, E. H.: *Sean O'Casey: A Bibliography of Criticism.* Macmillan, London, 1972. This covers O'Casey's books and plays, listing reviews of his books and of productions of his plays.

# The author of these notes

BARBARA HAYLEY is a Senior Lecturer in English at St Patrick's College, Maynooth. She was educated at Trinity College Dublin and the University of Kent at Canterbury. After a business career in London she was a Gulbenkian Research Fellow at the University of Cambridge, and a Fellow of Lucy Cavendish College. Her publications include *A Bibliography of the Writings of William Carleton; Carleton's Traits and Stories and the Nineteenth Century Anglo-Irish Tradition*; and York Notes on Gavin Maxwell's *Ring of Bright Water* and Jane Austen's *Emma* and *Mansfield Park*.